The Novels of V.S. Naipaul

The Novels of V.S. Naipaul

A Study in Theme and Form

Shashi Kamra

Distributed By
ADVENT BOOKS
141 East 44 Street
New York, NY 10017

Prestige

Published by
Prestige Books
3/28, East Patel Nagar, New Delhi 110 008
in association with
Indian Society for Commonwealth Studies
New Delhi

1990
ISBN: 81-85218-12-9

Jacket design by
3-A Corporation,
New Delhi 110 002

Phototypesetting by
data culture
New Delhi 110 065
Ph. 6431070

Printed by
Mehra Offset Press
New Delhi 110 002

Contents

Preface

The present study is an inquiry into V.S. Naipaul's fiction as an experiential recreation of the third world consciousness as it emerges into an anguished awareness of 'unimportance' in the modern world. The desire for 'importance' motivates Naipaul's protagonist. Trapped as he is in his situation, he struggles to release himself guided by notions of freedom, innate and acquired. As observed by the author a pattern of close relationship between the roles of the protagonist, narrator and writer creates not only a multivalent vision for the reader but suggests Naipaul's awareness of the complexity of his material. The interaction of these consciousnesses permits a facile conflation of contexts: philosophical, subjective and objective. Naipaul, recipient of most of the world's major awards for fiction, in his acceptance speech for the Bennett Award 1980, expressed his pleasure at the recognition accorded to his writings as a whole. And, the 1983 Jerusalem Prize for "The Freedom of the Individual in Society," awarded to Naipaul in tribute to "his noble vision of man's struggle for freedom and liberty," is a singular recognition of the relevance of his world view as projected in his writings.

Naipaul's fiction cannot be critically examined exclusively within any European tradition of the novel; criticism of fiction derives from the same social tradition as the fiction itself, and Naipaul's basic problem is the lack of any specific tradition.

The novels are, therefore, arranged under chapter-headings which are perspectival appraisals of the central theme and no chronological determination is intended.

Finally, the relationship between entrapment and freedom remains an open question. It is suggested that the concept of freedom, derived from the same metaphysical milieu as the experience of entrapment, leaves modern man suffocated by the intellectual atmosphere of the past, which is the reason why he is unable to see the present clearly or think dispassionately about the future.

The line of approach adopted in this study of Naipaul's fiction seeks to bring out his principal concerns as a novelist and thinker which suggest a remarkable exploration of contemporary man's situation made complex by his having to contend with entrapping metaphors of existence.

V.S. Naipaul:
A Profile of a Literary Radical

In his acceptance speech for the Bennett Award 1980, V.S. Naipaul expresses his particular pleasure at the recognition accorded to his writings as a whole. He feels that it is an acceptance of the relevance of his vision and his art. Naipaul has become a tradition. The interviewers of the *Newsweek* article of August 18, 1980, call him "one of the few original voices of his time. Today Naipaul stands as the master of the novel, a creative craftsman of such surpassing talent that Britain's leading literary critic, V.S. Pritchett, calls him "the greatest living writer in the English language." He has received most of the major awards for English fiction beginning with the first book he published: *The Mystic Masseur.*

The just but delayed recognition which Naipaul's genius is now receiving was accorded him by William Walsh much earlier. In his book *V.S. Naipaul* he says,

> Themes for him assume the forms of action and ideas appeal to him only in so far as they satisfy for him, as per Henry James, 'the appetite for the illustrational.' His vision is his own, unenervated by contemporary social cliches or political routines. . . . He is engaged with the stresses and strains we recognise as crucial in our experience now. His writing is nervous and present. This, together with the mixture in him of creeds, cultures and continents, with his expatriate career, his being able to practise an art in and of totally dissimilar worlds, all gives him a peculiarly contemporary quality.[1]

He further says,

Coleridge's words about Wordsworth are peculiarly appropriate to the nature of Naipaul's sensibility. He has the telescopic sight of the unattached observer, who is not only a creative observer, even an observer of genius, but one in whom the observation of others leads to analysis of self.[1]

Critics in their efforts to 'place' Naipaul fail to appreciate his 'apartness' and end up by fighting windmills. Most critics approach Naipaul with an external bias either literary, thematic (socio-political) or biographical.

He is viewed as a satirist who "makes his characters appear unnecessarily ridiculous,"[2] who has little sympathy with human failings, particularly those of the third world. His literary style is examined segmentally: the value of the absence or presence of a narrator in his individual works and the uses of irony and satire as distancing devices as well as an expression of personal distaste. Besides, there is a tendency to interpret and justify such criticism in terms of Naipaul's own pronouncements over a number of years without treating them as part of a body of literary thought and criticism.

The literary assessments of his work--satiric, ironic, farce--are backed by established literary conventions applied per se to assert the richness or otherwise of his novels. This reserved response to Naipaul contrasted with the critical success of other West Indian writers rests, ironically, on the fact that he 'relates his literature to life'; he never lets either get out of hand in his novels. His fiction and nonfiction shies away from the symbolic significance of a poem. Hena Maes-Jelinek writes:

My impression, however, is that his obvious contempt for the colonial society is typical of his attitude to men in general. . . . If Trinidad, as part of the province of El Dorado, did not come upto men's expectations, it is because they themselves never live up to their dreams.

Not all Caribbean writers look upon El Dorado as a myth which generated only disillusion and a second-rate way of life. Nor do they necessarily consider their history as something to be ashamed of. . . . The myth of El Dorado was given a new significance by such writers, who made it a symbol for a new quest.[4]

As Dickensian novels, these are supposedly a cruel arraignment of his own past social milieu.

Biographical criticism tends to flavour his life with his literature and vice versa. It becomes spicy, gossipy and simplistic, making no effort to grasp the imaginative expanse of Naipaul's mind and his capacity for empathy, by establishing close comparisons between incident and outlook. Keith Garebian writes:

> ... the plethora of direct comments on landscape in Naipaul's art indicates that the author is charting a mythology for the settings of his fiction and those of his own life. Landscapes are explored in order to provide characters with a real home, a true place of belonging so that they will not continue to be homeless wanderers unsure of themselves and their fates. But the mythology of the land is tinged with embarrassment, nervousness, hysteria, and pessimism--all products in some way of Naipaul's own history as a colonial with an ambiguous identity.[5]

The critics dismiss Naipaul in generalities. They see him as a superb writer of the comedy of manners, a man who writes about people as if they were "patients on the psychiatrist's couch."[6] He can neither be described wholly as a historian, a travel writer, a journalist, a novelist or a biographer. They seek to define him negatively and can be accused of applying the same techniques of questing into the unknown of which they accuse him. And so the critics continue to attack and praise him for the same reasons: that his work, encompassing a single unhappy vision of the contemporary world, 'lets man down.'

They fail to realize that the failures and disillusionments of his protagonists are presented as a necessary existential despair, (for it

11

is the only point at which man today touches his reality) which may become a turning point, a cause for change, in a world that lives life as a 'comedy of manners.' The latter appraisal comes out of a first and cursory reading of his novels.

Those critics who appreciate his work as a whole are however agreed that "At all events, he has achieved a mature literature."[7] John Updike begins his review of *The Loss of El Dorado* with the following unqualified admiration of Naipaul:

Never ask an artist to do the ordinary.[8]

He ends it critically:

For the fallacy of the primitive paradise, it seems to me, Mr. Naipaul wants to exchange that of the metropolitan paradise. This desire gives "The Loss of El Dorado" its bleak and caustic tone, yet also its persuasive sadness and the power of poetry.[9]

Sometimes this praise is grudgingly conceded:

In his peripatetic journalism, V.S. Naipaul is turning *into the prose-poet of the earth's destitute;* he is also becoming world-weary--or third world-weary, anyway. Perhaps this is the condition of the exile: compelled to travel, condemned to find nothing new.[10]

The only meaningful assessment of his art and vision, being without categories, can be made by divesting ourselves of literary terms and concepts and personal bias to 'sink' into the reaiity of the created world successively with the protagonist and the narrator and realize the differences between the two and their distance from Naipaul.

That a writer's work is bound to be influenced by his life is a worn out cliché. Such a statement needs careful and discriminate handling in order that biography should serve as an entry into the fictive world.

I would not hesitate to place Naipaul's despair in his experience of a lack of tradition. He is a major world novelist who has successfully created prose fiction focussed on societies without moorings. His fiction has an existential strength which redefines the established norms of the novel without destroying the latter. If he has not vanquished the fear of the "death of the novel" he has successfully kept it at bay.

Robert Hamner gently chides Naipaul's critics in his introduction to *Critical Perspectives on V.S. Naipaul:*

> When there are works so rich in esthetic and humanistic value as Naipaul's are, it is unfortunate that many readers and critics are put off by such peripheral concerns at the author's political affiliations, or the quality of his compassion.[11]
>
> In the final analysis, his predecessors, the sources of his material, and his political affiliations are not as important as the individual works, which must stand on their own merits. ... By putting his finger on elusive problems, foibles, follies, and vices, re-creating them within recognizable characters, he gives immediacy and comprehensible form to a reality which is otherwise too complex and expansive to grasp. This is no small achievement. Its magnitude is witnessed by the growing seriousness with which his work is being received by critics throughout the English-speaking world.[12]

V.S. Naipaul in an article published in *The Times Literary Supplement,* 4th June, 1964, reminisces on his earliest contacts with English literature after he had already decided to become a writer. "I went to books for a special sort of participation."[13] "I went to books for fantasy; at the same time I required reality."[14] "Literature, then, was mainly fantasy" because "the English language was mine; the tradition was not."[15] Naipaul here uses the word tradition in a very particular and precise sense: literary tradition and within that the tradition of the novel as an art form. He makes his context very clear by enumerating the great writers of the "realist" novel

13

in English and European literature--Dickens, Austen, Bronte sisters, Maupassant and Moliere--who formed his literary experience. Unable to appreciate the reality these writers portrayed, his imagination working uninhibitedly, such reading only delayed his personal realization of the "mind" of his own country which Matthew Arnold has stated as an essential for any great literature. It only succeeded in making him intensely aware of the intellectual vacuum in his society. The tradition that was not his was the particular social, political, philosophical structure of bourgeois society of England from the seventeenth century to the present day out of which the novel emerged and developed. Naipaul regrets this absence of a literary tradition as a handicap to a writer of fiction. For he can only write about his society; for every writer needs a "starting-point for further observation; . . . Every writer is, in the long run, on his own; but it helps, in the most practical way, to have a tradition."[16] His was a society without heroes. It was a multiracial, immigrant, slave, colonial society with the "drive and restlessness of immigrants." It was a stunted society with the forms of tradition and culture surviving but the core lost, submerged, destroyed: rendered meaningless and unimportant. Naipaul says: "To us, without a mythology, all literatures were foreign. Trinidad was small, remote and unimportant, and we knew we could not hope to read in books of the life we saw about us."[17] "My material had not been sufficiently hallowed by a tradition; I was not fully convinced of its importance: and some embarrassment remained."[18]

This anguishing experience of a lack of tradition remains the hallmark of his fiction. To practise his art with any degree of security he was forced to relate literature to life--to examine situations. He writes about peripheral, amorphous social groups without a discernible core, seemingly anarchic and chaotic, their very acceptance and adherence to traditional forms--their own, acquired or imposed--reveals their insubstantiality and hollowness rendering them easily destructible. He portrays most convincingly the anonymous man; his security lies in anonymity yet he is driven by the normal human impulse to leave a mark. His heroes are always in search of a more dignified life which becomes, for them, the essence of a full life. This search becomes a trap as the form it takes is repetitive of the power/domination drive which initially enslaved them. His protagonists/narrators come to rest in the awareness and actions of the contemporary artist/tramp: man is without a core. He realizes that the core (essence) of life can never be touched as, like a mirage, it recedes before an ever-widening consciousness; to live intensely in the present . . . is the acceptance of the futility of such a search. The final release is the discovery that to live a full life knowledge of the core is not necessary. Nietzsche, in *Thus Spoke Zarathustra*, says: "In each Now, Being begins; round each Here turns the sphere of There. The center is everywhere. Bent is the path of eternity."[19]

At no point does Naipaul suggest that man is not a spiritually aspiring being. He seems rather to say that such experience is not the lot of common humanity today. What passes for spirituality is magic, ritual and subservience to self-interest. This drive towards an abstract essence is the privilege of a few souls and ends in silence. Fiction, being based in material reality (conflicts, polarities, differences) Naipaul does not introduce silences into his works even through the back-door. Naipaul insists on need of a tradition, a myth, a history as an external starting point for the self in order for a man to become real: someone whose presence or absence is felt. If man is deprived of it he will search for it or create it. A sense of reality is more than awareness of actuality. It is a multivalent perspective acquired through varied experience. This is analogized in his novels as the protagonist's agonizing experience of the 'sense of place.' The 'sense of place' is the existential experience of the other, the 'Look' of Sartre represents the dialectical polarity to the hero or protagonist in a work of fiction. Yet, paradoxically, the protagonist's developing 'sense of place' leads, momentarily, to a timeless and placeless moment. This the protagonist/narrator experiences negatively as the void of despair or positively as the creative objectivity of the artist as God "above and behind his handiwork." In both cases the gap between the self and place closes and becomes as fine a distinction as that which Naipaul envisages as existing between truth and fiction. This is a kind of purification rite which

15

Naipaul's existential hero needs in order to return to the world. It is an individual personal experience, unable to be shared or poeticized.

Naipaul's anguish over the absence of a philosophical-literary tradition parallels the experience of loss which underlies modernist art--Imagism, Surrealism, Dada, Existentialism and the Theatre of the Absurd.

The modern temper is characterized by introspection, anxiety and insecurity and radical doubts about human freedom and dignity. Determinism in human affairs is given a scientific, positivistic basis by Marx, Freud, Nietzsche, and anthropological and linguistic approaches to human life which emphasize reality as structures rather than essences. Philosophically Existentialism fills in the gap left by a revolt against those values which characterized and reflected transcendental systems, particularly Christianity and Hegel's idealistic logic. In a world without God, or God only as a figurehead, the Nietzschean Dionysiac r ian, the artist, revels in his powers as the revelator of life. In the Existential writings of Kierkegaard, Heidegger and Sartre the artistic self, though diminished, yet retains dignity and sanity as it strives to achieve its values through faith or commitment. It is in the Expressionistic drama of Cocteau and the Absurd drama and fiction of Beckett that alienation, angst, fear, solipsism, self-wounding, man trapped in a meaningless universe, wandering goalless or in circles of habitual action, that the modern temper is fully realized. The experience of loss of meaning in nature and in personal and social history is dramatized as nightmare. The immediate context of the development of the tortured modern consciousness has been forcefully stated by John Press in his introduction to *A Map of Modern English Verse:*

> Two world wars, the reintroduction of torture by governments generally reckoned to be civilized, the scientific planning of genocide, the deliberate crushing of the individual by totalitarian states, the eviction of millions of families from their homes, the outbursts of irrational violence and of racial

16

hatred in the great cities of the world, the possibility that *homo sapiens* may destroy himself--all these factors have lent urgency to the question 'What is man?' It is the question which haunts modern English verse.[20]

Naipaul has succeeded in transforming a personal (socio-political) and a literary problem into a dialectic of his fictional technique. Tradition, history and legend, with him, does not assume mythic, archetypal and spiritual proportions as it does with Eliot in his poetry. Neither is it an absolute cultural and religious promise of a happy life which the disillusioned modernists were forced to discard. In Naipaul's work there is the same overpowering significance of history and tradition as is present in T.S. Eliot's:

> Tradition is a matter of much wider significance. It cannot be inherited, and if you want it you must obtain it by great labour. It involves in the first place, the historical sense. . . . This historical sense, which is a sense of the timeless as well as of the temporal and of the timeless and of the time temporal together, is what makes a writer most acutely conscious of his place in time, of his own contemporaneity.[21]

Within the context of his early fiction tradition, women; marriage and 'a sense of place' spell a historical reality which is an actual impediment to success (money, owning a home, political power, holding a high government office or any position assuring status) in the colonial setting. In his later fiction tradition, 'a sense of place,' women, become imaginative, emotional projections of the literary sensibility. The writer's experience of them fluctuates between the imaginative and the actual; his emotional reactions to them possess the ambivalent quality of human love towards a desired person: torn between the desire to possess and be possessed and the fear of losing personal identity, of non-being, with its accompanying impulse to escape.

Tradition, then, in all its aspects: as the trap of a static life, as the promise of the future, as the desired and the feared, as the

17

controller of man's vision and action becomes internalized as 'mood,' which being the expression of the total personality at any particular moment is incapable of analysis and hence of being captured. In his fiction it becomes a major objective correlative for the existential anguish of loss and impermanence, the effort to overcome it and the inability to do so except temporarily: it is the subjective and sensible apprehension of the metaphysical entrapment of the self.

The question 'What is man?' leaves modern art open-ended, stressing the norm of infinite possibility and subsuming its nihilism. Rejection of a feeble tradition released vast resources of creative vitality which expressed itself in vigorous experimentation with form and the use of language. Joyce, Stein, Virginia Woolf, Gide, Proust, Sartre and Camus are some of the major literary figures of the early 20th century who in this manner legitimized the novel as an art form, though Henry James was the first innovator to realize the possibilities of the novel. In talking about them Robbe-Grillet in his *For a New Novel* says,

> such writers know that the systematic repetition of the forms of the past is not only absurd and futile, but that it can even become harmful: by blinding us to our real situation in the world today, it keeps us, ultimately, from constructing the world and man of tomorrow.[22]

But nostalgia for a lost world remained a powerful motivation to modern creativity. Construction of mythologies or personal landscapes and the use of mythological material to reveal modern sensibility testified to the need for a framework of reference: for meaning to become meaningful. These two opposite pulls on the sensibility of the artist constituted the energy of the modern movement.

The modern artist's ultimate dependence for his material on his personal experience has resulted in artistic awareness of commitment to political and sociological reality as well. The artist's release from the restraints of tradition is accompanied by restriction

18

through choice of political and sociological ideologies. W.H. Auden believes that "The mere making of a work of art is itself a political act."[23] And it is the politically generated cultural, social and economic reality of Third World countries which shape and circumscribe Naipaul's fictional concerns. Choice becomes a necessity for, as he says, "we are not all brothers under the skin."[24] And we are not yet ready to live as citizens of the world. This realization emerges in the novel as man's heightened sense of helplessness in a chaotic and hostile world.

Naipaul's artistic sensibility can be linked at all points with literary modernism. His art, however, is not the consequence of a revolt from and a rejection of a literary tradition. There are no ghosts to be laid or standards to be met. In this sense it is a freer and more inclusive art. Robbe-Grillet would envy him his freedom:

> The writer himself, despite his desire for independence, is situated within an intellectual culture and a literature which can only be those of the past. It is impossible for him to escape altogether from this tradition of which he is the product. Sometimes the very elements he has tried hardest to oppose seem, on the contrary, to flourish more vigorously than ever in the very work by which he hoped to destroy them; and he will be congratulated, of course, with relief for having cultivated them so zealously.[25]

Tradition does not have a possessive hold on him hampering his style and sensibility. He has a haunting dread of imitation and yet a compulsion to write. He is able to generate a new form to express his awareness of his material. He has attempted a greater spatialization, objectification and materialization of time than has so far been attempted to highlight the 'here and now' anxieties and tensions of colonial sensibility.

Naipaul's existential need to link literature to life enables him to see beyond the novel as an art form, a major direction which modernism took. Without formal commitment to a theory of art he can manipulate novel forms through parody and pastiche without fear of sacrilege, in his personal quest of man's responsibility to the world he lives in. In this his philosophical sensibility parallels that of post-World War II artists, the post-modernists, whose focus shifts from a study of man 'en situation' as the centre of the universe to a study of the universe as such where man and objects, man as individual and social, have equal rights, and can only be known, if at all, 'en situation.' The underlying question is: what is the relationship between truth, fiction, history, reality and the artist's relations to these as material and form for the novel. Finally it filters down to questioning the artist's inviolability and infallibility and art as the vehicle of truth. The artist is now writing for himself, to extend his personal vision. Art is an extrasensory experience. All the senses, functioning together, become a new sense and add to the artist's subjective experience of the world. Yet the contrary vision is there as well. The artist cannot keep his finger out of the pie that is the world. In post-modernist fiction the writer is often presented as the imposter, impersonator, juggler or magician: all roles signifying degrees of unreliability. Yet the implication is there that the artist, in his quest for coherence, is best able to achieve a many-dimensional, multifaceted personality which functions harmoniously precisely because it incorporates the principles of flux, flexibility, change and materiality; this to some extent neutralizes the artist's accepted unreliability.

Post-modernist fiction communicates to the reader a deeper nihilism than that of the Existentialists for it excludes and excuses no one, least of all the writer from its purview. To man's sense of being dwarfed and overpowered by an experiential awareness of an unstable metaphysical and natural universe is added the relentless inhuman domination of man by machine so dynamically prophesied by D.H. Lawrence, in his fiction. A redemptive vision remains only on the margin of contemporary fiction and so unlike Lawrence, the technique which expresses this vision is a reductive one: to place man as an object in a world of objects, knowable at the surface or just below.

Two quotations, one from Sartre and the other from Robbe-Grillet, juxtaposed, present a possible fresh perception about the relationship between metaphysics, fictional technique and the artist's vision of himself in the anti-novel. Sartre's definition of the anti-novel:

> an attempt to undermine the accepted forms of the novel from within. The anti-romans preserve the appearance and contours of the novel; they are imaginative works which present us with fictive characters and tell us their story. But it is for the purpose of better deceiving us: their aim is to make use of the novel in order to challenge the novel, to destroy it before our eyes while seeming to construct it, to write the novel of a novel unwritten and unwritable... they call attention to the fact that we live in an age of reflection and that the novel is in the act of reflecting on itself.[-]
>
> It is God alone who can claim to be objective. While in our books, on the contrary, it is a man who sees, who feels, who imagines, a man located in space and time, conditioned by his passions, a man like you and me. And the book reports nothing but his experience, limited and uncertain as it is. It is a man here, now who is his own narrator, finally.[17]

These two quotes together with Herbert Marcuse's philosophical proposition for a change of direction in contemporary world politics are subtle indicators of the direction of Naipaul's fiction:

> However, underneath the conservative popular base is the substratum of the outcasts and outsiders, the exploited and persecuted of other races and other colours, the unemployed and the unemployable. They exist outside the democratic process; their life is the most immediate and the most real need for ending intolerable conditions and institutions. Thus their opposition is revolutionary even if their consciousness is not. The fact that they start refusing to play the game may be the fact which marks the beginning of the end of a period.
>
> It is only for the sake of those without hope that hope is given to us.[28]

21

The artist is subsumed under the generic term man; the artistic sensibility is only one possible extension of the frontiers of man's consciousness; art not only provides an understanding of but is itself, as R.R.K. Singh says in *The Mimic Men*, an extension of personality.

This study attempts to demarcate the literary field within which Naipaul as a writer and visionary has developed. The values of the Western literary tradition within which he is situated are recoverable. The anguish over the lack of tradition expressed in literary terms is the expression of a deeper existential loss which is irrecoverable and irreplaceable. It is not the loss of rejection or of something forgotten but of total amnesia of one's historical heritage and a refusal to accept one's actual parents as the only evidence of the self. Camus, in *The Myth of Sisyphus*, expresses man's experience of absurdity in similar terms:

> But in a universe that is suddenly deprived of illusion and of light man feels a stranger. His is an irremediable exile, because he is deprived of memories of a lost homeland as much as he lacks the hope of a promised land to come. This divorce between man and his life, the actor and his setting, truly constitutes the feeling of absurdity.*

Naipaul's protagonist is not only a stranger but an orphan, unrelated, in a world of relationships, of which he is keenly aware. The exercise of power both as inhuman brutality, perpetuating the oppressor/oppressed syndrome, as well as the creative and constructive aesthetic life appears to be the privilege and possibility of societies secure within a tradition. Insecure societies can only hope to imitate and thus remain second and third rate cultures. But further investigation reveals that the greater mobility of the rootless man makes the search for an authentic and creative life in the present economic and political world situation easier, provided he has the sensibility. That is the trap. For, according to Naipaul, sensibility is not purely a matter of heredity. It is the result of breeding within

22

a viable tradition. It establishes one's sense of continuity with the past with its implication of a larger family tree for the self. There are traps within traps. For the polarities tradition and freedom from tradition must co-exist within the same person if he is to live a full life.

Identifying the problems of the writer with those of the man Naipaul feels the necessity to define a personal concrete and creative metaphysics against the given and imagined frame of reference of Hindu India. Naipaul spent a year in India. He wrote a most thrilling and factual account of his existential journey into the self, into his past, into the mythical land of his childhood and as he sees it now, of the disparity that forever exists between the imagined and the actual: *An Area of Darkness*. What is inexpressible to him he expresses in a quotation from Charles Darwin's *Voyage of the Beagle:*

> Only the other day I looked forward to this airy barrier as a definite point in our journey homewards; but now I find it, and all such resting places for the imagination, are like shadows, which a man moving onwards cannot catch.[30]

He fails to enmesh India in understanding and having consciously rejected her tradition his experience of her remains partial. The loss is his and he traces it to his attitudes and temperament. Yet he knows moments of emotional identification in his nostalgic appreciation of certain traditional practices and rituals. The final struggle is with himself--between his upbringing and his unacknowledged inheritance. This brings him to India again and another lover's quarrel results in *India: A Wounded Civilisation,* a book which outrages and antagonises Indians. His attitude is more pliant and involved: "India is for me a difficult country. It isn't my home and cannot be my home; and yet I cannot reject it or be indifferent to it; I cannot travel only for the sights. I'm at once too close and too far."[31] According to an interview by Shyam Ratna Gupta printed in *The Hindustan Times Weekly,* Sunday, May 31, 1981, Naipaul has said: "I should like to settle down in Bombay and rediscover my identity by losing myself in the millions of India.'' This should satisfy those critics who assert that Naipaul has a superior and detached outlook on life and who see no development of vision in his novels. Hindus should understand this statement as evolving out of the two passionately critical books about India which they find hard to accept. Is it another paradoxical statement about existential loss becoming the grounds for identity and stability?

Besides these two accounts of his travels to India he has documented other equally involved journeys to other third world countries in *The Middle Passage; The Caribbean Revisited* and *Among the Believers:An Islamic Journey.* In the former he is on familiar ground. In a relaxed, racy first person style he places the causes for continued unimportance of these former slave islands, now politically independent, not only in their rising populations and economic insecurity but also in their own shortcomings: divisive tendencies and disunity--the lack of a larger vision. One can sense the pain beneath the words:

> I had seen how deep in nearly every West Indian, high and low, were the prejudices of race; how often these prejudices were rooted in self-contempt; . . . Everyone spoke of nation and nationalism but no one was willing to surrender the privileges or even the separateness of his group.[12]

Among the Believers is in every sense an important travel document being a full-length account of a relatively unknown yet vital region of the Third World; these nations have always been important culturally and commercially. The Muslim peoples have usually been studied as contributors to world culture and power but not on their own ground. Naipaul examines the unique human quality of the Muslim: his despairs and aspirations; his understanding of the self and the rest of the non-believing world. In his inimitable personal manner he states the strengths and shortcomings of Islamic Fundamentalism as a political experiment:

> No religion is more worldly than Islam. In spite of its political

24

incapacity, no religion keeps men's eyes more fixed on the way the world is run. . . . I thought I could see how Islamic fervour could become more than a matter of prayers and postures, could become creative, revolutionary, and take men on to a humanism beyond religious doctrine: a true renaissance, open to the new and enriched by it, as Muslims in their early days of glory had been.▪

A Turn in the South, Naipaul's latest travel book, describes his peregrinations through the Deep South of the USA--Mississipi, Tennessee, Alabama, Georgia, the two Carolinas and Atlanta. He travels not just for the sights and sounds but as he says he 'travels on a theme.'

This time he explores disaffection as a way of living and thinking among the poor whites and blacks--communities on the periphery of the monolithic mainstream of American culture of which they desperately seek to be a part. Among these people, who see themselves as victims of a hostile past, Naipaul discovers a 'sense of place', a sense of home--of being actively linked to their own piece of earth. They have some place to go back to when defeated.

Naipaul is lyrical in his assessment of these sons and daughters of the soil as he ponders on their Biblical simplicity--their firm sense of material worth and personal dignity. Race issue is what he had been interested in but as he says he ''didn't know then that that issue would quickly work itself out during the journey, and that my subject would become that other South--of order and faith, and music and melancholy--which I didn't know about, but of which I had been given an intimation in Dallas.''▪

The Overcrowded Baracoon and Other Articles and *The Return of Eva Peron with the Killings in Trinidad* are collections of articles, written over a fifteen year period, of serious, reflective journalism, with a focus on evidential and existential truth. Here the resemblance between the two books ends. The first book brings together interviews of and by Naipaul, book reviews, first hand impressions of the Indian mind, and his views on the Japanese and

25

the American mind through observation and dialogues with their leaders--political, literary and financial; besides this are included his early impressions of England and the meaning they held for him. Written between 1958-1972 they reflect his youthful impatience with and scorn of all forms of fraudulent living.

The articles in *The Return of Eva Peron* (1972-75) are a more compassionate survey, the length of long short stories, of the political and personal power of Eva Peron, Mobutu and black power leader Michael de Freitas, covering contemporary Jamaica, Argentina and Zaire, all three considered as colonial cultures. These articles focus on the distress of a people which combined with the support of interested power groups in the West, take advantage of this malaise to support the leadership of those local people who possess no other qualification except that of a distorted and ambitious self-vision and an eye to opportunity. Naipaul writes:

> Much of the population is superfluous, and they know it. Unemployment is high but labour is perennially short. The physical squalor, the sense of a land being pillaged rather than built up, generates great tensions; . . . but the situation is well suited to the hysteria and evasions of racial politics. . . .
>
> Malik, an operator acting always in the racial cause, found in Trinidad his perfect camouflage."
>
> In the early Peronist days she was promoted as a saint, and she is now above Peronism and politics. She is her own cult; she offers protection to those who believe in her. Where there are no reliable institutions or codes or law, no secular assurances, people need faith and magic. . . . Desolation always seems close in the Argentine vastness: how did men come here, how have they endured?"

The last piece on Conrad, extremely fine literary criticism, brings him alive, Naipaul's autobiographical narration making it as exciting as an adventure story.

> Conrad's value to me is that he is someone who sixty to

26

seventy years ago meditated on my world, a world I recognize today. . . .

Nothing is rigged in Conrad. He doesn't remake countries. He chose, as we now know, incidents from real life; and he meditated on them. (210)

A Flag on the Island is similarly a collection of imaginative writing between the years 1950 and 1965. The short pieces explore the imaginative, thematic and stylistic resources available to Naipaul, the locales varying from Trinidad to London to an unnamed island, presumably in the Caribbean, realizing its value only as a base for American troops during World War II. No unity is sought but the title of the novella conveys the metaphorical suggestion that the pieces converge on the desire for identity with dignity. Many of the incidents and characters presented in isolation appear as part of a design in his later fiction.

Miguel Street along with *A Flag on the Island,* in the light of his later novels, can be regarded as the brickwork of his personal literary tradition. The 'grey dailyness of living' as well as the frightfully superficial release such people seek is evoked through the metaphorical use of landscape and language as well as the experimental manipulation with points of view and the degree of the narrator's presence in the narrative. We see in *Miguel Street,* in initial form his lasting concern with the sources of wholeness (unity in difference) in art. The street acquires a warm, sincere personality through the combined visions of the young first-person narrator and his much older, philosopher friend, Hat. We acquire Hat's world view through the narrator. Naipaul juxtaposes the inexplicable resilience of the human spirit with the meanness of life in the slum, making the narrator's escape seem logical and reasonable.

Hat said, 'Life is helluva thing, You can see trouble coming and you can't do a damn thing to prevent it coming. You just got to sit and watch and wait.'[27]

Naipaul's fiction and non-fiction have not only placed him as

27

the 'greatest living writer of the English language' but as one of the world's most sincere and progressive humanists who refuses to bluff others and himself. In his own words:

> The new outlook fashioned by science implies a new outlook of man. They're going to realize that you have to respect man because he's man and that it's wrong to hand out charity.[38]
>
> The 'Third World' notion is itself a cliché. I feel there's a great universal civilization at the moment which people would say is Western. But this has been fed by innumerable sources. It's a very eclectic civilization and it is conquering the world because it is so attractive, so liberating to people. . . . The mistake of Western vanity is to think that the universal civilization that exists now is a purer racial one. It's not the preserve of one race, one country, but has been fed by many.[39]

The open-ended, multi-dimensional, autotelic novel as the only means through which he can fully explore his inherited as well as created multi-context situation is for Naipaul an existential necessity. For through it he "seeks to realize some of the inexhaustible ambiguities of the human heart confronting fundamental issues"[40] by beckoning us "into appreciation of ineffable feelings going beyond the analysis."[41] Naipaul intends, through his novels as the "resting-places of the imagination"[42] to convert literature into an "equipment for living."[43] Panichas, in *Reverent Discipline*, quotes Sartre, "the written work can be an essential condition of action, that is, the moment of reflective consciousness."[44]

Naipaul's novels develop from a fundamentally existential position. Underlying all his fiction, like the refrain of a song and circumscribing his novelistic vision, is a view of man which derives from western existential philosophy particularly as interpreted by Sartre. Without a practising belief in a transcendent power and authority man can still overcome his alienation and achieve an authentic life through imagination and commitment. "What all people want, some without being aware of it, is to be witness to their time, their lives, and above all to themselves."[45] Metaphysical

28

alienation is compounded by an isolation which is the consequence of the urban, industrial values of contemporary society and that engendered by historical circumstance. Naipaul presents critical awareness of alienation as necessary and healthy but not necessarily permanent. It is related to the sense of entrapment, the desire to be free and finally to a desire for human community and a personal sense of social responsibility. His rootless protagonist/narrator does not relish his condition as a man adrift.

His novels are not panoramas nor realistic appraisals of social or personal life but attempts to illuminate "an area of darkness"[46] as he has known it: the sense of being disconnected from the sources of power. He does not hesitate to state the relationship between his style and purpose, clearly defining the context of his novels and the responsibilities of the novelist. Meaning in his novels is a consequence of this limitation of context imposed by the purpose of the novelist as revealed through his style. In a *Newsweek* interview in August 1980, Naipaul said in reply to the question:

> "How do you see yourself now after sixteen books?"
> "As a maker of books. I'm pleased if people recognise not just that they are well-written, but appreciate the way they are constructed. I am happy when a book written twenty years ago still has some meaning for people."[47]

A week later Naipaul, in an article about him in *The Times of India*, is reported as saying:

> I'm not concerned with style for its own sake. I try to destroy the rhythm of the prose if I find it. I'm concerned with letting each thing add to the other, trying to say exactly and clearly what I mean. It isn't a problem of seeking a new form, but of finding the reality of the situation.[48]

His novels coalesce the form of the novel of manners with that of the novel of sensibility in such a way that each develops a moral perspective on the other. This blending of the biographical and the autobiographical modes creates that sense of urgency, "which takes us beyond what we witness and becomes a symbol for aspects of our own experience."[*] The reader grasps the 'reality of the situation' as an experience through the pervading mood of the novel. For it is only through mood that Naipaul can dramatize organically the unity of a reality which is essentially complex, ungraspable, dangerous and human. Mobility, complexity, relatedness and order are interdependent human necessities which as realized potential eliminate categories and polarities. For him the image of contemporary man as the Aryan horseman riding to the edge of the flat world can never be final.

It is the mood which holds together the various structural elements of the novel--the dramatic, reflective and descriptive--by becoming the ground for the selection of episodes and incidents from the life of the protagonist by the narrator. It is the emotional atmosphere of the novel which permeates and holds together the elements of experience (time, space and man) and yet underlines its insubstantial nature. The mood acts as the medium through which echo all the pressures of a personal/historical past as they press down and mould the narrator's/protagonist's responses to a present situation.

The mood is built up by an "orchestration of perceptions"[30] on these selected situations through the multiple perspectives of the novel on the multiple thematic polarities. In his fiction the existential polarities of tradition and personal meaning, the psychological polarities of the literal and the literary, the unidimensional and the multidimensional man, the social polarity of small town and metropolitan life, the political polarity of the colonizer and the colonized (oppressor and oppressed) coalesce to create the experience of man trapped, fragmented and rootless struggling for release through a self-realizing order. It is the precise placing of images and phrases--their repetition in changing contexts--that builds up the rhythm and nuances of the novels. "There is always an aura of mystery, of strangeness, awakened by the immanence of obsessive images and by incantatory language."[31]

Naipaul uses dramatization, reflection, description, the centre of consciousness, the stream of consciousness and the third person omniscient narration to create an overwhelming mood in the novel structured out of an accumulation of minor irritations which become the premonition of a major crisis.

Meaning as the mood of the novel is the reader's simultaneous apprehension of the written and the unwritten. It is the tension between the realized and the unrealized within the novel. Hence meaning as a consequence of the writer's style can never be, for Naipaul, merely an "arrangement of words."[22] The unit of perception for him is the scene: "I say things in visual images, sometimes with sentimental touches. I put construction first. Every paragraph must have its colour, its rhythm."[23] The image of the incomplete house, the ship-wrecked man, the hurricane, the water-hyacinth choked river, the expatriate and the tramp--of some kind of "elemental complexity,"[24] of the failure of relationship--haunt his fiction.

The mood that haunts his novels is that of existential despair. It is similar to existential absurdity: of anguish at living in an unrelated meaningless world: in a void. Naipaul sees it as a moment of despair gone out of man's control: as a critical situation which suggests the possibility of a reorientation in the life of the protagonist and the narrator:

> all the activity of these years, existing as I have said in my own mind in parenthesis, represented a type of withdrawal, and was part of the injury inflicted on me by the too solid three-dimensional city in which I could never feel myself as anything but spectral, disintegrating, pointless, fluid. The city made by man but passed out of his control break down the negative reaction, activity the positive: opposite but equal aspects of an accommodation to a sense of place which, like memory, when grown acute, becomes a source of pain.[25]

This depiction of despair as an arrested, enlarged moment in the life of the protagonist which triggers off a reaction in the narrator suggests that a critical situation is a part of an ongoing process of life which becomes so 'in the circumstances.' For out of this definition of despair emerges the possibility of authentic action as well as hope of community and relationship, of the comic note in the novels. It is what is left unsaid that provides the positive thrust which counterbalances the image of despair.

The limitations of the context limit the sensibility and the extent of imaginative suffering of the protagonist and narrator. The context which limits their movements is contemporary. The acute political, social, cultural, and economic uncertainties of the Third World is their milieu. The alert colonial personality experiences dislocation and dislodgement of the self from its insufficient background and seeks a fresh identity. It becomes aware of material opportunities in terms of self-interest or is a moral, intellectual sensibility astray seeking a wider and more creative context. The perpetual state of insecurity which motivates his third world expatriates becomes a critical human awareness of ageing associated with retirement in the context of urban English culture in *Mr. Stone and the Knights Companion.*

Naipaul's narrator then wrests meaning out of an essentially meaningless situation as he responds imaginatively to the protagonist's dilemma through a perpetual sense of wonder and a desire to remake the world:

> To the conquistador where there were no wonders there was nothing, place was then its name alone, and landscape was land, difficult or easy. . . .
> Untouched by imagination or intellect, great actions become mere activity; it is part of the Spanish waste. El Dorado becomes an abstraction; deaths become numbers.[14]

He examines the role of memory, imagination, history, tradition, and extent of self-awareness of the present as organizers of a personal vision, which can be given aesthetic and experiential expression in the novel. The novel becomes the vehicle of man's ontological need for a personal order.

Therefore, within the context of Naipaul's fiction meaning,

32

like tradition, acquires thematic dimensions. It polarizes tradition as the experience of absurdity: either as habitual patterns of seeing the world or as free-wheeling fantasy. From both of these situations the protagonist and narrator feel obliged to dissociate themselves as they fail to give a sense of purpose, of an actual order or pattern. Meaning becomes identical with the authentic life witnessing the reality of the self as relationship through willed action. The stories his father wrote about Trinidad, writes Naipaul,

> provided a starting point for further observation; they did not trigger off fantasy. Every writer is, in the long run, on his own; but it helps, in the most practical way, to have a tradition. The English language was mine; the tradition was not.
> Literature, then, was mainly fantasy.[17]

Hence "I sought continuously to relate literature to life."[18] He seeks to fuse the word "Jasmine" with the scent of the flower.

Naipaul takes this initial personal definition and through the multi-dimensional structure of his novels transforms meaning and tradition as existential categories into meaning and tradition as continuum: as an unfolding of human potential. Meaning as continuum is man's awareness of an expanding, mobile and complex context. Meaning as a probing into man's contexts necessarily subsumes tradition revitalizing it as an element of the contemporary situation. Any aspect of the context ignored is a meaning attenuated, an imperfect relationship. It becomes a condition for the stasis of repetitive behaviour inducing the feeling of entrapment.

Meaning, as a source of power and community energises the latent links between man and his environment so that man's "meditation in the presence of otherness"[19] is also "man's continuing search for a basic orientation in his situation."[20] The existential narrator, reflecting over the protagonist, seeks links (areas of concordance and discordance) between social and subjective meaning through empirical action which verifies the fact of a common humanity.

Within his novels Naipaul, his protagonists and narrators all

33

share in varying degree, a common existentialist and physical heritage. All three are rootless men whose feeling of unimportance expresses itself as a desire to leave a mark. Political independence exposes the false security engendered by the colonial experience leaving them as mimic or hollow men:

> It seemed to me that those of us who were born there were curiously naked, that we lived purely physically. . . .
>
> And really, looking at that place, land-locked from the sea and shut off from the land by the precipitious slopes of mountains, it was difficult to believe in the existence of any neighbourhood. It was still, complete, unknown, and full of a life that went on stealthily with a troubling effect of solitude; of a life that seemed unaccountably empty of anything that would stir the thought, touch the heart, give a hint of the ominous sequence of days. It appeared to us a land without memories, regrets, and hopes; a land where nothing could survive the coming of the night, and where each sunrise, like a dazzling act of special creation, was disconnected from the eve and the morrow."

But their search for principles of action, and their drive towards wider contexts manifests their potential as individual human beings. It is a critical situation in the psyche of such nations and is experienced by its alert, intelligent and aggressive members as a personal dilemma. Their picaroon society with its materialist orientation, opportunism, adaptability, tolerance, laughter--all indicative of the capacity for quick change--is easily moulded; it discloses its spiritual assets to its more penetrating members. As Satendra Nandan says:

> Virtually all of Naipaul's writings deal with the predicament of the 'unanchored souls.' In a dozen works, Naipaul's vision has never faltered, indeed it has widened, with a sense of urgency and immediacy, into a more universal fate, moving into other cultures, other lands, other peoples. However, the

34

underlying, unifying reality is always the same. That he has made the Caribbean experience an integral strand in the pattern of human condition is his signal achievement.[a]

All three emerging from a common context and meeting in a situation which is equally comprehensible to all three, the startling differences between their personalities and their seemingly irreconcilable situations makes each book a unique experience. For the reader it emerges as the experience of distinct personalities separated in time and place yet able to meet in a catalytic existential situation. To understand this simultaneous presentation of distinctiveness and wholeness the multiple contexts and multivalence of his novels can be defined as the thematic relationship between three diverse personalities: between the protagonist and the narrator, between these two and Naipaul. And if the narrator's complex response to the protagonist's situation is taken to represent the fusion of three points of view, there are at least six perspectives on each novel.

It is the actual situation of the protagonist in each novel which regulates its structure. He is given detailed treatment in each novel evolving as a rounded character through the multivalent vision of the narrator. The latter, in developing the story chronologically, gives it the dimensions of physical and psychological reality. The protagonist grows into a man who finds some meaning, however slight, in his life which enables him to accept his failures and disappointments with greater equanimity. It is him the reader sees grappling with defeating and destroying circumstances, refusing to yield to them and say 'no' to his sense of self. He is basically a simple, straightforward man in the contemporary cosmopolitan context hardly worth noticing or talking about except among friends and acquaintances and then to be forgotten. At the most the protagonist is a local celebrity whose achievements and fame are as thin and brittle as his personal identity and the status of his country as a new member of the comity of nations. As a local hero he might receive newspaper notices. But in newly-independent countries such celebrities spring up like mushrooms in the rainy season and disappear as fast. As such he appears as an isolated instance of a common case. It is the protagonist in Naipaul's novels who "affirms the homely sanctity of the commonplace, where there can be an acceptance of the imperfection of all things, human action chief among them."[43]

The essential experience of the narrator is of one who is acutely aware of the objective existence of the 'other' as a missing human awareness of life, of being diminished by its absence and of trying to relate to it in terms of a dialectic of the self. Naipaul does not allow the self-conscious narrator to lose his grip on the narrative. The reader never loses his perception of the narrator's satiric/ironic vision within each novel. Thus the presence of the existential narrator is crucial to the meaning for it is he who draws the protagonist into the centre of human affairs from his position at the edge of existence. It is the narrator who forges the links, however tenuous because totally subjective, between the protagonist's personal situation and that of the world of politics and history, enlarging the context of the particular situation:

> Until Naipaul wrote his novels the indentured labourer was featureless.... But it is Naipaul's writings which have given these 'dregs of humanity' a place in the educated conscious-ness of the world community. For the first time the face of the coolie acquires distinctive features which have the power to disturb a conscience.[44]

It is only the ironic, existential, supposedly uncommitted and unbiased narrator who can dramatize the situation and vision of the third world protagonist as trapped and static, and also imply his possibilities for freedom:

> To arrive at this sense of a country trapped and static, eternally vulnerable, is to begin to have something of the African sense of the void. It is to begin to fall, in the African way, into a dream of a past--the vacancy of river and forest, the hut in the brown yard, the dugout--when the dead ancestors watched

36

and protected, and the enemies were only men.[14]

Analogously it reflects his own state as well. His is the sensibility constantly alert to crises and danger with the moral courage and freedom to make choices and decisions to act.

In his insistence on subjective empirical truth, he devalues the authoritarian power-oriented societies of the world. He is the perpetual anti-colonial and revolutionary. His hunger for 'experience' makes him value his homelessness and rootlessness as assets in his enterprise to know the world to which he relates through the imagination and language. His mind ranges over the whole universe of discourse--myth, gesture, dream, silence, logic, symbolism and structuralism. The subjective and the objective are both possibilities of the narrator through irony, self-reflection and projection. He enables the reader to see the protagonist as he sees himself and as the world (represented by the narrator) sees him with his personal assessment leaning towards the latter view as is evidenced by his satiric commentary on the protagonist and his performance.

The roundedness of the protagonist and the other characters is a consequence of the existential narrator's commitment to empirical truth: he is compelled to express what he sees and as he sees it. For him reality is subjective. Naipaul presents him as the polar opposite of the protagonist within the context of each novel. This explains his varying roles to meet the demands of the context. His is the existential, sophisticated, literary sensibility, rational, scientific, humanistic and Westernized providing a foil and contrast to the uni-dimensional, literal, simple, colonial, authoritarian personality of the protagonist. Both are alert, intelligent, sensible, imaginative and mobile but both subscribing to certain assumptions trap themselves in certain static situations.

The existential narrator's limited sensibility, his satiric and superior attitude to the protagonist allows Naipaul to control the reader's attitude to the novel and its meaning by shifting his attention to the situation. The extensive attention that the protagonist receives combined with the anonymity of the narrator, his lack of antecedents in the novel and his satiric negative involvement with the protagonist precludes him as the exclusive conveyor of the meaning of the novel. He remains the 'I' or unnamed and implicitly present through his tone and purpose to highlight the protagonist as the mimic man.

The situation as dramatized by Naipaul is of a materialist world where people are essentially alienated for lack of a transcendent reality. It is a situation which has about it an air of isolation; of people moving on their personal axes, of lives related to the objective world only at its edges, accidentally. He visualises the world in terms of a barracoon; "But tranquillity recedes. The barracoon is overcrowded; the escape routes are closed. The people are disaffected and have no sense of danger.''[46] The least and the most that life offers as a means of survival is the life of the tramp or the artist. The tramp, as the uncommitted citizen of the world, exposes himself to hostility as a scapegoat for aggression and violence. The artist finds commitment difficult because of the complexity of his vision and the elusiveness of contemporary reality:

> The ancient artist, recording the life of a lesser personage sometimes recorded with a freer hand the pleasures of that life: the pleasures of the river, full of fish and birds, the pleasures of food and drink. The land had been studied, everything in it categorized, exalted into design. It was the special vision of men who knew no other land and saw what they had as rich and complete.[47]

Incidentally, the necessary, subjective, unverifiable vision of the existential narrator allows Naipaul to present his interpretation of the situation as a question requiring continual meditation and pondering. This view of the novel as a perpetual question is similar to what Robbe-Grillet has to say about Art:

> Art is life. . . . Art cannot exist without this permanent condition of being put in question. But the movement of these evolutions and revolutions constitutes its perpetual renais-

sance."

Naipaul's fiction answers to the demands of a literature of engagement, of commitment, without proliferating the energies of the novel form. His purpose controls his aesthetic form and circumscribes his novelistic vision. He controls the situation to be evoked by narrowing and pinpointing it actually and metaphysically. He has succeeded in tickling men's minds by very compelling portrayals of men without identity and roots determined to survive at all cost: to build a home.

Naipaul's fiction is designed to convey to the reader the experience of a particular situation in which alienation and absurdity occur in contemporary life. His fiction can also be considered as a tracing of links between the actual and the artistic world of the writer. It deals primarily with the facts of confrontation between the third and first worlds in the colonial and post-colonial situations from the 1950s onwards. The situation is defined as a realisation of inferiority and backwardness and a desire for equality and modernity. Naipaul's third world is delimited to those colonies whose societies are composed of immigrant peoples. Imported as labour these people eventually possess only the external structure of a homogeneous civilization. Without any roots in the country in which they live they are more vulnerable to exploitation than those colonial societies with ancient indigenous cultures. A large part of the world's population has been so convinced of its inferiority that it accepts Western values as absolute; subservience is their natural response to life.

Naipaul's fiction renders this vision dramatically through the multivalent outlook of the narrator stressing the psychological, the subjective and the individual: the third world man desires to enter the first world. In his effort to do so he rejects or loses whatever third world reality he possesses and is yet unable to enter the first world. But he does succeed in a kind of existential understanding of the human need to survive and the different ways taken. He presents psychological facts not as ontological but as having a cultural/ historical bias and therefore capable of change through reinterpre-

39

tations and reorientation. A hesitant and barely positive blueprint for a world culture does emerge from his fiction. He sees the possibility of human equality in a rejection of those institutions which make subservience a necessity and virtue; all forms of exploitation of human resources to satisfy the needs, natural and created, of any privileged section in society. This subservience takes its primary shape in the institution of marriage and in family life, in having a home symbolised by ownership of a house--a promise of wholeness, protection and personal authority. This desire for a home, according to Naipaul, reveals a lack of awareness or a deliberate turning away from contemporary reality. The third world man can play the traditional role of manhood only in his home, as master, protector and creator. However, this home, where he has his roots, becomes a trap for him. It accentuates his alienation from community life and responsibility. The security it offers is similar to the state of death. It is necessary but not sufficient to live subjectively: it becomes a form of refuge and fantasy. Man must move out of his home, discard the past as present or convert it into the past in the present, travel light and if possible achieve a sense of self-realisation through constructive/creative action.

The hazards and disillusionments of this life far outweigh its possibilities but it provides sufficient room to make a personal, positive gesture in the interests of community through a sympathetic grasp of the other's situation. This vision is dramatized in the prologue and epilogue of *In a Free State*. The sympathetic third person narration of the tramp's situation in the Prologue comes to fruition in the Epilogue in the first person narration of the action taken to defend the dignity of the Arab urchin who has not had the chance to know of his possession and loss of it. In his novels the situation is more complex. It is the narrator's act of narration which rescues him from the literal world. But the narrator remains unreliable. The protagonist carries the weight of the contemporary situation.

Naipaul effectively combines the use of the autobiographical and the biographical modes of fiction to reveal the simple one-dimensional protagonist as he clamours incessantly to be free, his

40

growth in awareness as a sense of loss or life in a vacuum, and the necessary fight for survival. This permits him to switch between first and third person narration to convey the sense of wholeness of reality as residing in complexity, and that of continuity in personality through ambiguity and paradox. It enables him to present the development of sensibility from the literal to the literary as a consequence of interaction between man and his varying contexts (past/present, subjective/objective, historical/political, actual/ideal, place/time, concrete/abstract) without sacrificing the literal man's need for chronology or allowing the literary man's fantasies and extreme subjectivism to affect the credibility of the story or the form.

This balance between the literal and the literary is ably maintained by the existential narrator's relation to the protagonist. The former, though not the central, is yet the crucial figure through whom the novelist develops the concept of multivalence as the art of life and of the novel. Multivalence is achieved through a simultaneous expression of closeness and remoteness between the protagonist and narrator. Sympathy and distance are seen as natural as well as artistic phenomena. The relationship between the narrator and the protagonist is well-defined either as cultural and familial identity (as an ambivalent father-son, or the reverse situation) as in the Trinidad novels, or cultural-literary identity as in *Guerrillas* and *Mr. Stone and the Knights Companion*.

The narrator and protagonist express their identity in terms of awareness of 'place.' It is claustrophobic and concrete; it provides security and stability; their desire for freedom is expressed negatively as an escape from the literal prison and ultimately 'place' and then 'placelessness' become the conditions of freedom. The narrator by 'placing' the places in his life is able to reduce their threat as permanently imprisoning conditions; by objectifying places he becomes master of them. His revelations, the critical moments in his life, have very definite concrete surroundings. It is only when he is away from them that he is able to understand the full significance of the relationship between perception and place.

'Sense of place' becomes the psychological as well as the

literary projection of anonymity defining the parameters within which his novels develop; the literal and the literary. 'Sense of place' coincides with `the truth of the self,' the 'golden landscapes,' with having or not having a tradition, or a home; it defines the third world mental landscape and its lack of a sense of time, or the historical sense. In man's natural understanding of himself place takes precedence over time. For the third world character 'sense of place' time is his most poignant experience of racial/social/intellectual inferiority; he uses place to explain it and it becomes his refuge from total destruction in a time-oriented world. It is being a slave, literally or metaphorically, living in geographically isolated, historically unknown places, it is role-playing and it is the desire to be a sophisticated man of the modern world. It is the final knowledge that he has been on the wrong track and bewilderment and anguish as a consequence of his momentary inability to see an alternative. It becomes, through the novel, the reassertion of life and continuity--the fundamental human equality--through writing. The book becomes a stable, irrefutable though temporary, identity--it occupies a place.

Becoming modern is growing in awareness of the value of time as concrete reality: ageing, waste, absurdity. Time becomes the abstract, questioning dimension for the literary consciousness--an expression of fear at man's inability to hold the clock back. For modern material reality time, life and death have become irrelevant except as philosophical/literary speculation. Time in human literary awareness has always been concretized through place (city of God versus the city of Man) and so time by being made eternal has been made impotent by man. Naipaul assigns awareness of time to the narrator rather than the protagonist. The narrator's moments of revelation occur through blending of the protagonist's 'sense of place' with the narrator's sense of time. Time and place are destructive when not balanced by eternity: man is trapped in his context. The fullness of the narrator's experience lies in his appreciation of such moments as aspects of a whole life. The language of revelation is the language of experience: the emotional impact of a particular time and place coalescing as the mood of that person in

42

that situation--'da-sein.'

The protagonist's mood of dissatisfaction with his present place, and his compulsion to escape through moving away, the narrator's overpowering fear at the loss of all footholds on life: by a subtle interplay of moods Naipaul creates for the reader an awareness of the terror which underlies the apparently smooth third world situation and which erupts unexpectedly into uncontrollable and unexplained violence. Naipaul's third world stretches its boundaries to include all people who are physically, mentally and emotionally displaced.

The definitive and literal use of words, phrases, sentences and images in discrete contexts concretizes the experience sought to be conveyed. For the protagonist, repeated use of words in different situations can indicate a limited experience of language, a limitation of intellect or imagination, limited knowledge and terms of reference. They conjure the reality of a man unable to transcend his material, fragmented existence except in rare moments of achievement and self-satisfaction.

For the narrator contextual juxtaposition of the protagonist's particular expressions of life enables him to gather up the fragments in order to recreate a personality pattern. Ironically, he remains unaware of its temporary and fictive nature. His feeling of wholeness achieved as precise understanding of the interaction between the subjective and the objective life enables him to accept his life, which he sees as Life, as it is.

Naipaul stretches particular words, phrases, sentences and images throughout each novel, and from novel to novel not only to ensure his particular vision but to give language and thought a body. Though the contexts conflate they never merge and become one. The narrator never loses self-awareness. Words have meaning in situations and understanding of situations involves the ability to use language, "to restore to the living event all of its value."

The underlying tone of his novels, deriving from the first person narrator, is existential. He sees the truth of modern life as an interplay between man's sensibility, situation and language. Structurally the novels emphasize the importance of the subjective, sensible life as the foundation for identity. They explore the possibilities inherent in man's imaginative and linguistic capacity to create a world out of the experience of absurdity. This narrative world is the culmination of the narrator's possibility for the time being. It leaves him emptied out, alienated and facing the void; he experiences the necessity for a fresh start.

However the drift of the narration is away from expansion of the self as a consequence of alienation and towards the recovery of the objective world through action. Communication is not purely a subjective, imaginative, fictive enterprise but a genuine interchange and relationship between the subject and the object. Alienation in Naipaul's novels is relative distance between the self and the other: the polarities resolve themselves into a continuum. Philosophically the novels carry the reader beyond the vision of the narrator to reaffirm, by widening our context, the concept of community and action as the identifying realities of an individual's personality. Naipaul, by making the narrator create in detail the rich texture of the protagonist's life with all its struggles, failures and vanities, presents the reader with an argument in which one cannot doubt where his bias lies. The narrator through all his intense alienation cannot ignore the objective existence of the world and his relationship to it: his senses vouch for it.

The understanding of the distance between the narration and the novel becomes an assessment of the relationship between the narrator and Naipaul. Naipaul presents himself in the fiction as an extension of the context within which the narrator narrates his tale. This extension is the presence of the ironic/poetic sensibility which brings the whole world as place and all of time (past/present/future) into the novel.

> The modern world, after all, cannot be caricatured or conjured away; a pastoral past cannot be re-established."

Therefore the narrator is not a mask for Naipaul but a distinct individual created by him. In omniscient third person narration *(A House for Mr. Biswas, The Suffrage of Elvira, Guerrillas, Mr.*

Stone and the Knights Companion) the narrator's presence is felt through the satiric tone of the novel. The narrator's effort to reduce the protagonist to pocket-size becomes indirectly a means of self-inflation. The protagonist resists these pressures which will level him and emerges as a full-bodied individual whose agonies are so genuine that their meagre causes drift into the background.

The scenic, descriptive and reflective aspects of the narrative cohere being related facets of the central sceptical vision of the narrator. But in each novel there is at least one scene which is entirely dramatic: there is no commentary preceding or following it. It comes somewhat as a surprising conclusion to the narrative. It is the point where the narrator disappears either by identification with the protagonist or is annulled by his more powerful presence as in *A Bend in the River* and *The Mystic Masseur* respectively. Here Naipaul the author steps into the open and takes over the novel from the narrator. Naipaul and the narrator meet existentially in the dramatisation of a sense of personal failure as well as a certain awareness of the ambiguous relationship between failure and success.

The existential reality of the novel for the reader as a study of ahistorical, historical and poetic tensions takes shape through a study of its beginnings and endings and by relating the titles, subtitles, epilogues and prologues to the actual narrative. These arbitrary divisions of the narrative are not an indication of the craft of the narrator but that of Naipaul the author. They materialise him as the author's presence in his fiction; the author intrusive by implication. They have not merely a descriptive but a functional relationship within each novel becoming an aspect of its ironic/poetic vision. In the final dramatic scene the reader stands apart from Naipaul the author and the narrator for he is not allowed entry into their subjective conditions. Therefore the note of hope in a possible reorientation of thought and action is a conclusion of the reader as he engages critically in the developing relationship between the three: protagonist, narrator and Naipaul the author. Naipaul the author adheres strictly to the standards of objectivity prescribed by himself. The views of Naipaul the man may be echoed by his narrator; in that case the man is a creation of the author.

NOTES

1. Williams Walsh, *V.S. Naipaul* (Edinburgh: Oliver and Boyd, 1973), p. 3.
2. Ibid., p. 15.
3. Robert Hamner, ed., *Critical Perspectives on V.S. Naipaul* (London: Heinemann, 1979).
4. Hena Maes-Jelinek, "The Myth of El Dorado in the Caribbean Novel," *The Journal of Commonwealth Literature*, VI/1, June, 1971, p. 116.
5. Keith Garebian, "V.S. Naipaul's Negative Sense of Place," *Journal of Commonwealth Literature*, 10/1, pp. 23-4.
6. Martin Amis, "More Bones," review of *The Return of Eva Peron with the Killings in Trinidad*, *New Statesman*, 4 July 1980.
7. Hamner, p. 125.
8. *Ibid.,* p. 153.
9. *Ibid.,* p. 158.
10. Martin Amis, "More Bones."
11. Hamner, p. xxix.
12. *Ibid.,* p. xxx.
13. V.S. Naipaul, *The Overcrowded Barracoon and other Articles* (Harmondsworth: Penguin, 1976), p. 26.
14. *Ibid.,* p. 25.
15. *Ibid.,* p. 27.
16. *Loc. cit.*
17. *Ibid.,* p. 24.
18. *Ibid.,* p. 27.
19. Herbert Marcuse, *Eros and Civilization* (London: Routledge and Kegan Paul, 1956), p. 122.
20. John Press, *A Map of Modern English Verse* (London: Oxford University Press, 1977), p. 4.

21. T.S. Eliot, "Tradition and the Individual Talent," *The English Critical Tradition*, Vol. II, ed. S. Ramaswami and V.S. Seturaman (Madras: Macmillan, 1978), p. 169.

22. Robbe-Grillet, *For a New Novel: Essays on Fiction*, trans. Richard Howard (Freeport, N.Y.: Books for Library Press, 1970), p. 9.

23. W.H. Auden, *Dyer's Hand and Other Essays* (London: Faber, 1964), p. 88.

24. *The Overcrowded Barracoon and other Articles*, p. 15.

25. Robbe-Grillet, p. 9.

26. Donald Heiney and Lenthiel H. Downs, *Continental European Literature: Essentials of Contemporary Literature of the Western World*, 2nd ed., (Woodbury, N.Y.: Barron's Educational Series, 1974), I, p. 269.

27. Robbe-Grillet, p. 139.

28. Herbert Marcuse, *One Dimensional Man* (London: Routledge and Kegan Paul Ltd., 1964), p. 257.

29. Heiney and Downs, I, p. 295.

30. V.S. Naipaul, *An Area of Darkness* (Harmondsworth: Penguin, 1979), p. 27.

31. V.S. Naipaul, *India: A Wounded Civilization* (Harmondsworth: Penguin, 1979), p. 8.

32. V.S. Naipaul, *The Middle Passage: The Caribbean Revisited* (Harmondsworth: Penguin, 1975), pp. 253-54.

33. V.S. Naipaul, *Among the Believers: An Islamic Journey* (London: Andre Deutsch, 1981), p. 167.

34. V.S. Naipaul, *A Turn in the South* (Viking: Penguin, 1989), p. 25.

35. V.S. Naipaul *The Return of Eva Peron with the Killings in Trinidad* (Harmondsworth: Penguin, 1981), p. 59.

36. *Ibid.*, p. 162.

37. V.S. Naipaul, *Miguel Street* (Harmondsworth: Penguin, 1971), p. 91.

38. "V.S. Naipaul in Paris," *The Guardian Weekly*, 125/4, July 26, 1981.

39. "The Master of the Novel," *Newsweek*, August 18, 1980.

40. Harry R. Garvin, "Introductory Essay," *Makers of the Twentieth Century Novel*, ed. Harry R. Garvin (Cranbury, New Jersey: Associated University Press, 1977).
41. *Ibid.*
42. *An Area of Darkness*, p. 27.
43. George A. Panichas, ed., *The Reverent Discipline* (Hawthorne Books, 1974), p. 6.
44. *Ibid.*, p. 12.
45. Edith Kern, *Existential Thought and Fictional Technique* (London: Yale University Press, 1970), p. 100.
46. *An Area of Darkness*.
47. *Newsweek*, August 18, 1980, p. 38.
48. *The Times of India*, August 24, 1980.
49. *The Return of Eva Peron with the Killings in Trinidad*, p. 214.
50. *Ibid.*, p. 203.
51. Harry Garvin, pp. 250-51.
52. *The Return of Eva Peron with the Killings in Trinidad*, p. 203
53. *The Guardian Weekly*, 125/4, July 26, 1981, p. 13.
54. V.S. Naipaul, *The Mimic Men* (Harmondsworth: Penguin, 1977).
55. *Ibid.*, p. 52.
56. V.S. Naipaul, *The Loss of El Dorado* (Harmondswoth: Penguin, 1977), pp. 19-20.
57. *The Overcrowded Barracoon and other Articles*, p. 27.
58. *Ibid.*, p. 28.
59. *The Reverent Discipline*.
60. *Ibid.*
61. James Joyce, "A Portrait of the Artist as a Young Man," *The Portable James Joyce* (New York: Viking), p. 255.
62. "Conrad's Darkness," *The Return of Eva Peron with the Killings in Trinidad*, pp. 205-06.
63. Satendra Singh, "The Immigrant Indian Experience in Literature: Trinidad and Fiji," *Awakened Conscience*, ed. C.D. Narasimhaiah, (New Delhi: Sterling), p. 348.
64. Murray Krieger, *The Tragic Vision* (Chicago and London: The University of Chicago Press, 1966), p. 266.

65. Narasimhaiah, pp. 354-55.
66. "A New King for the Congo: Mobutu and the Nihilism of Africa," *The Return of Eva Peron with the Killings in Trinidad*, p. 196.
67. *The Overcrowded Barracoon and other Articles*, p. 309.
68. "Circus at Luxor," *In a Free State* (Harmondsworth: Penguin, 1978), p. 241.
69. Robbe-Grillet, p. 159.
70. *India: A Wounded Civilization*, p. 41.

Political Reality and its Predilections:
The Mystic Masseur; The Suffrage of Elvira; The Mimic Men

In the three novels *The Mystic Masseur, The Suffrage of Elvira* and *The Mimic Men* Naipaul concerns himself with the political reality of Trinidad just before and after independence. Independently the three novels examine different aspects of the reaction to political independence of the individual and the group. Each novel dramatizes a particular feature of Trinidad's inability to go back to colonial security or to generate a national identity thus emphasizing its political insignificance. Each is an arrested moment of reality which is not a final assessment of the situation.[1] Together they can be seen as the testament to an emerging maturity of vision. They discuss the politics of mutual self-deception which flourishes unhindered in a nonpolemical society. Such a system gives the impression of self-sufficiency until a crisis reveals its hollowness and unreality: being isolated and self-isolating, not seeking its links through inertia.

The Mystic Masseur is an account of a typical aspirant to power and prestige gravitating to politics as the supreme possibility. Emphasis is on Ganesh's qualities of personality: his assertiveness and his alertness to opportunity indicating his greater sensitivity to his environment. He dominates easily in an environment which is lethargic and easy-going. He is the prototype for Naipaul's instinctually successful men, the Nazruddins of the world, who know when it is time to move on; they intuitively avoid the existential trap of extreme situations when choice becomes irrelevant. *The Suffrage of Elvira* highlights the political situation as it prevails in a typical village in Trinidad. The narrative develops the nuances of community life which focus the lack of community feeling. It is a dialogue in which the participants are clearly identified into the insider village group with an overall sense of self-benefit who treat Harbans as the outsider antagonist. The narration develops as a game of bluff in which the roles are reversed. Harbans as exploiter of votes is fully exploited by his electorate till his despair at heavy personal loss becomes the tone of the novel; the narrator's awareness is of waste of opportunity and possibility. In these two novels the narrator has deliberately desisted from establishing a historical base. Ganesh and Elvira, removed from the purview of history, become objects of bitter satire. This is the attitude of the outsider to a world which he considers as closed, unqualified and essentially absurd. In *The Mimic Men* the autobiographical account gives the protagonist both a historical as well as an existential context and thus redeems the previous static reality as a study of the relationship between political power and human nothingness, oppressor and oppressed, colonizer and colonized.

The implications of the novels emerge from an understanding of the nature of the engagement of the protagonist and narrator with the political situation specifically during the first two elections (1946, 1950) based on adult universal suffrage to the democratic parliament just before and following independence from British Colonial Rule. The narrator identifies the destiny of the country with the personality of its emerging political leaders. For there is no political machinery which can absorb the shocks of individual conduct:

> Nationalism was impossible in Trinidad. In the colonial society every man had to be for himself; every man had to grasp whatever dignity and power he was allowed; he owed no loyalty to the island and scarcely any to his group. To understand this is to understand the squalor of the politics that came to Trinidad in 1946 when, after no popular agitation, universal adult suffrage was declared. The privilege took the population by surprise. Old attitudes persisted: the govern-

ment was something removed, the local eminence was despised. The new politics were reserved for the enterprising, who had seen the prodigious commercial possibilities. There were no parties, only individuals. Corruption, not unexpected, aroused only amusement and even mild approval.[1]

Political power embodies the colonized's dream of power, possession and self-realization. The validity of this dream is questioned by the narrator. Paradoxically, though distanced from the drama of the novel in time and place, he is emotionally entrapped within the situation and hopes for release through objective understanding-- watching Garbage behind the pillar. The narrator's irony and satire is a reflection on the unquestioning and greedy mimicking of patterns of behaviour of the colonial which the achievement of political independence and democracy implicitly rejects. This mimic behaviour is generated as much by a natural human response to the contemporary world--to leap across centuries--into roles esteemed by the world powers as to a lack of indigenous institutions and thought systems. The essential fact that the colonial is now incorporated into the subjective reality of the colonized has to be accepted in order to contend with the reality of the situation. The polarization of awareness along a continuum of consciousness which ranges from simplicity to sophistication (literal to literary) dramatizes the emergence and existence of the third world protagonist:

> We began in bluff. We continued in bluff. But there was a difference. We began in innocence, believing in the virtue of the smell of sweat. We continued with knowledge, of poverty and power. The colonial politician is an easy object of satire. ... It is that his situation satirizes itself, turns satire inside out, takes satire to a point where it touches pathos if not tragedy. Out of his immense violation words come easily to him, too easily.... The support he has attracted, not ideal to ideal, but bitterness to bitterness, he betrays and mangles: emancipation is not possible for all.[2]

Combining a scientific humanist outlook with a romantic existential sensibility, the narrator identifies with his protagonists in their moment of failure. He presents it as a historical time-bound situation thus minimizing the inherent element of absurdity. Their personal loss measured against their mimicked concepts of success explains Trinidad's continuing colonialism, dependence and unimportance. Independence instead of making it a responsible member of the world community has brought it the tourist boom. It, like Ganesh, is the entertainer of the world--the buffoon. Yet the moment of existential despair which Harbans expresses succinctly, "Elvira, you is a bitch," is the moment of release from single-minded formulas which entrap a man in repetitive action. Multivalence, sophistication, awareness of the other thrusts itself humiliatingly on his consciousness. Focussing on this moment as the pivot of his narrative choices the narrator is able to tone down the protagonist's mood of despair at irreversible personal loss and his own awareness of Trinidad's failure to meet the challenge of equality and modernity which independence and democracy have offered.

These novels may be considered political to the extent that, as Molly Mahmood says in *The Colonial Encounter*, all colonial novels arise from the novelist's sense of political pressure, and also because the protagonist sets his heart on the western polis as the enchanted city which will release him from the drabness and drudgery of his semi-urban existence.' The three novels under consideration dramatize the period of transition from colonial rule to self-government. The turbulence of this period is the consequence of the loss of the colonial order with nothing to replace it except borrowed forms and concepts which are manipulated by personalities motivated by the historical fear of non-existence. It is in R.R.K. Singh's words "chaos on which order has been imposed." Politics and government is an experiential phenomenon. The more responsible members of this society suddenly become conscious of their lack of experience--the best is missing. It has no leaders to bring it to maturity. What Naipaul says in *The Loss of El*

Dorado about the Venezuela of the early 19th century is true of Trinidad today:

> Spain had suddenly withered away; and Venezuela, cut off from Spain, was being shivered into all its divisions and subdivisions of race and caste. But it was not the revolution Governor Hislop or Miranda had expected. It was the loss of law. The pacific, deficient colonial society had become bloody. Spain was now seen to be more than its administrative failures. It was, however remotely, a code and a reference that the colonial society by itself was incapable of generating. Without such a reference obedience, the association of consent, was no longer possible.[4]

However these are not political novels in the usual sense of the term. The political background does not become a metaphor for philosophical, psychological and social elaboration of life. They also reveal that politics as ideology or government by consent does not exist in Trinidad either in fact or in knowledge.[5] It is never a political decision to contest election to the governing bodies. Electioneering is viewed in a social context--a form of participation in public life which creates the opportunity for success: financial and social. It is the area of widest scope for self-fulfilment with the least demands on talent and qualification. It was the first area of power which the colonial had to submit to the colonized unequivocally. Trinidadians had retained a confused racial and cultural memory but no political memory whatsoever. The political situation is defined only through the narrator's ironic vision; he first presents it as the protagonist's idealized golden landscape of opportunity and then contrasts it with his own awareness of it as chaos and disorder:

> I had never thought of obedience as a problem. Now it seemed to me the miracle of society. Given our situation, anarchy was endless, unless we acted right away. But on power and the consolidation of passing power we wasted our energies, until

the bigger truth came: that in a society like ours, fragmented, inorganic, no link between man and the landscape, a society not held together by common interests, there was no true internal source of power, and that no power was real which did not come from the outside. Such was the controlled chaos we had, with such enthusiasm, brought upon ourselves.[*]

Existentially, then, politics, like marriage, is defined as a need for order.

Nothing mocks the lack of politics in Trinidad more than the protagonist's accidental entry into it: by virtue of money, brains and opportunity rather than choice and commitment. The central situation in each novel is the experience of alienation from what he now considers a hostile society which so far had seemed a supporting system. For in his novels the protagonist as politician expresses the Trinidadian's greatest conflict with objective reality. It is the other which cannot be fantasied away and must be contended with. It is the faceless enemy that cannot be identified and killed. It makes its insistent demands on the individual to come to terms with it. Even Ganesh, the greatest bluffer in Naipaul's fiction, comes up against situations to which he must submit. He can only huff and puff at his humiliation as M.L.C. when he is invited to the Governor's dinner but he cannot deny it. It is his first experience of cultural shock--the golden landscape turning to land. In *The Mimic Men*, Singh analyses the causes for political failure as they relate to life on Isabella. And the answer, of course, is that politics and simplicity do not go together. The 'island politician' is a contradiction in terms and at best is an expression of 'political anxiety' rather than 'political awakening.' At this given moment the Trinidadian cannot rise above caste and race alignments to grasp his national essence.

The protagonists of these novels realize the self only through political failure. Such failure for an island politician becomes not only the 'point of no return' but is also a dead end. He cannot move forward either. He must learn to live in an 'as is where is' condition. The trap manufactured out of the colonial condition is strengthened by the colonized's inability to perceive its structure as it inheres in

55

his personality and environment. He just moves instinctively against restraint. Survival requires a deliberate effort to order experience through distancing beginning with the self and relating it in many ways to external reality. The process itself and the aesthetic perception it enables, provide a sense of release from this chaotic purgatory. The urge for survival makes the narrator examine the life of his protagonist; multivalence becomes a way of understanding which must precede purposive action. The narrator, questioning the chronological assertions of the narrative, converts dogmatic reality into flux.

This political despair of the protagonist as experienced absurdity provides the narrator with an entry into the very particular Trinidadian sensibility. Through it alone can he hope to make the reader aware of the essential simplicity and literalness of a colonized mind without a concrete past or a promising future, product of a system which recognizes only its market value, living out an isolated fantasy of fulfilment which rivals the amorphous subjective trapped existence of Beckett's protagonists--unable to live or die.

The study of the mind of the 'island innocent' makes mutual dependence a condition of growth as well as of entrapment, placing the highest possibility of man as a sense of responsibility for the self through awareness of the other. Authoritarian Hamm in *Endgame*, his despotism compensating for his extreme dependence, deliberately and cruelly eschewing human relationships as sources of pain, making himself into an object, is yet unable to still the restlessness of his mind. Painkillers provide temporary relief against both ennui and imagination. Without drugs his humanity asserts itself, however reluctantly, as he cannot prevent his imagination from constructing stories and responding appreciatively to the rhythmic flow of words. However this last outpost of humanism falls prey to absurdity as it becomes a drug to combat loneliness. As all vicious drugs it further alienates by reducing the need for communication. Naipaul's narrators, being simple men, never travel so far.

Naipaul's use of the narrator to focus the thematics of Trinidadian politics or the tragic lack of a national creative consciousness not only brings to the forefront the literal, grasping natural leader of his apathetic community but also enables him to present, by contrast with the ironic narrating sensibility, this sensitive intelligent man as an "innocent" who, unlike the former, has no intellectual resistance to change. For the sceptical narrator, over-conscious of the protagonist's failings and single-minded behaviour which gives the impression of a lack of profundity, direct action is almost impossible. His multivalent awareness becomes not a mode of action but of withdrawal. Both the protagonist and the narrator become failures within the terms of political reference. Naipaul, the author, controlling the action and thought of both the protagonist and the narrator, projects for the reader the awareness of a people adrift, rejected at home and abroad. The sense of total failure of the aspirants to political leadership is accompanied not only by a sense of immediate nothingness but a sense of continuing failure which will haunt all endeavour and will alloy all success.

The debate initiated on the meaning of politics evolves into the poetic image of men trapped and helpless to transcend the context of their own needs and desires in a hostile environment. Destructive anger is a temporary release from frustration. The aesthetic life which enables a man to control and order his chaotic experience through narration is the more constructive vision of Naipaul's narrators.

The Mystic Masseur and *The Suffrage of Elvira* have their setting in rural Trinidad with Port of Spain providing the stepping stone to the metropolis which is London. The protagonist of *The Mimic Men* is a native of Isabella which resembles Trinidad in all details. All three Caribbean island landscapes--warm, humid, sunny and fertile--are defined and reduced by the larger contrasted consciousness of sophisticated London which remains on the periphery of every Trinidadian's vision. London, as the capital of material and cultural success, provides the distinct signals which guide the subconscious and conscious thinking of Naipaul's protagonists and heroes--Ganesh, Harbans and R.R.K. Singh. These are essentially rural settings with a commercial bias. All the people that matter in Naipaul's novels have the experience of labouring for the benefit of another, of necessity, being at the losing end. The narrator's presence and bias is evident from the beginning of each novel in the manner in which he is able to suggest physical and intellectual poverty in the midst of plenty. The people, immersed in physical labour and material existence, the world of challenges far removed, are content to live their circumscribed lives requiring nothing of themselves or their surroundings: the minimum level of survival becoming the maximum limit of possibility.

It was a long drive to Ganesh's, more than two hours. He lived in a place called Fuente Grove not far from Princes Town. Fuente Grove--Fountain Grove--seemed a curious name. There was no hint of a fountain anywhere, no hint even of water. For miles around the land was flat, treeless, and hot. You drove through miles and miles of sugar-cane; then the sugar-cane stopped abruptly to make room for Fuente Grove. It was a sad little village.[7]

When he saw the women he thought of them only as objects he must try not to hit, and he didn't stop to think how strange it was to see two blonde women forcing red American cycles up Elvira Hill, the highest point in County Naparoni, the smallest, most isolated and most neglected of the nine counties of Trinidad.[8]

From the top of Elvira Hill you get one of the finest views in Trinidad, better even than the view from Tortuga in South Caroni. Below, the jungly hills and valleys of the Central Range. Beyond, the south, the sugarcane fields, the silver tanks of the oil refinery at Pointe-a-Pierre, and the pink and white houses of San Fernando: to the west, the shining rice-fields and swamps of Caroni, and the Gulf of Paria; the Caroni Savannah to the north, and the settlements at the foot of the Northern Range.

Harbans didn't care for the view. All he saw about him was a lot of bush.[9]

We were in the area of swamps. Sodden thatched huts, set in mud, lined the road. It was a rainy day, grey, the sky low and oppressive, the water in the ditches thick and black, people everywhere semi-naked, working barefooted in the mud which discoloured their bodies and faces and their working rags. I was more than saddened, more than angry. I felt endangered. My mood must have communicated itself to Cecil's father, for at that moment he said, 'My people.'

And now I was disappointed. I imagine I had expected more passion and more pain. But I kept my thoughts to myself and merely said, 'Why can't they give them leggings?' 'They' were the Stockwell estates, whose overseers' houses, tall concrete pillars, cream concrete walls, red corrugated-iron roofs, presently appeared, rather close together, with no gardens to speak of and as bare of trees as the sugarcane fields in which they were set. Miserable crop![10]

The Mystic Masseur is a very exact expression of the narrator's views on the contemporary Trinidadian hero--the politician. A parody of the log cabin to White House success story, for the sense of nationhood that inspired the fathers of democracy is totally missing, misunderstood or lauded, he is essentially alone and self-involved, acting more in a world of fantasy than showing crucial awareness of vital issues. The novel is hence as much the story of Ganesh as that of the unnamed narrator. He appears in a dual role: as the first person existent in Ganesh's life, a fact which proves crucial to both of them and establishes the subjective counterthrust to the objective biography, and the third person omniscient narrator of that biography. They share a common landscape but belong to different generations. The narrator, now a young student in England, meets Ganesh for the second time in his life as the leader of the Government delegation from Trinidad to England. Ganesh's gesture of non-recognition and denial reveals his hollowness: his suppression of all sense of loyalty to his past in a desire to fill out a role whose significance he has not grasped. Stunned, the student asserts his existence and retaliates by exposing Ganesh. The narrative winds its way through the issues of Trinidadian identity-- independence, politics, community--as it is viewed by one who is very conscious of his nationality. The epilogue is titled 'A States-man on the 12.57' and it stresses the fact of the narrator's awareness of himself as a foreigner in England:

In the summer of 1954 I was at an English university, waiting for the results of an examination. One morning I got a letter from the Colonial office. A party of Colonial Statesmen were in Britain for a conference, and would I be willing to entertain a statesman from my own territory?

What he is not aware of are the underlying tensions, uncertainties, frustrations of his inherited colonial past which he also shares with Ganesh:

Ganesh preferred not to remember what happened the next day when he was taken to school. The old boys laughed, and although he had not worn the khaki topee, he felt uncomfortable in his khaki suit. Then there was the scene in the principal's office: his father gesticulating with his white cap and umbrella: the English principal patient, then firm, and finally exasperated; the old man enraged, muttering, 'Gaddaha! Gaddaha!' (16)

This past surfaces when Ganesh ignores his individual existence and treats him as a colonial would behave with a Trinidadian--one below notice. Unable to assimilate this blow to his self-esteem which he experiences as a betrayal of a trust he in turn betrays Trinidad by exposing Ganesh for the picaroon he is and describing him as being representative of his society. The narrative simultaneously becomes a revaluation of the background from which he has evolved. Thus able to distance himself through Ganesh he arrives at a negative self-realization. This significance of the narrative is implicit in his sympathetic portrayal of Ganesh as a young man. The earlier part of the story is occupied with Ganesh as an ambitious and independent young man, yet idealistically and poetically inclined with a driving passion for books. He asserts his independence of thought again and again, rejecting his superstitious, materialistic and garrulous society. But he soon realizes that it is through this society only that he can realize his freedom from it. And so we see him submitting to its demands in order to use it to further his own ambitions. We see a man for whom his society provides no alternative patterns of a free life-style, for which even as he uses it he develops a distaste. His callous treatment of Ramlogan, his father-in-law, exemplifies his treatment of Trinidad. Even his autobiography, *'The Years of Guilt,'* is an indirect denial of Trinidad for he attributes his success only to the 'hand of Providence.' So that the narrator and Ganesh both meet as representatives of a society they both reject in their rejection of each other.

Naipaul, in dramatizing this mutual involvement of Ganesh and the narrator, enables the reader to realize the existential experience of each as differing because of the different sense of time and place--historical as well as existential (moulded by success and defeat respectively). Ganesh is seen as a man who moves ahead only by rejecting loyalties and responsibilities. He feels free with a new name, a new profession, unhampered by his wife or friends and the world before him. We see the paradox of his freedom. He has a name which is not his--Ganesh Ramsumair is altered to G. Ramsay Muir; a profession in which he is a puppet--he is less qualified to be an M.B.E. than he was to be a masseur; as a man he is truly adrift without the loyalty of Leila and Beharry to support and encourage him. The narrator, in revealing him as a charlatan has only succeeded in evoking our sympathy for him. By linking his private sensibility to his public career Ganesh's roguery appears as an element of his 'innocence': his 'self-cherishing' and his 'self-regard'; he accepts praise and flattery as his due. These terms Naipaul uses repeatedly to characterize a trait which acts as a pitfall to sincerity towards others yet constitutes a kind of faith. This innocence can become a condition of change provided the impetus is present. Ironically the narrator's progress as student is halted as he attempts to reconstitute Ganesh's colonial sense of success to present it as an awareness of national loss.

The slant of the narrative reveals the narrator's awakening to the fact of an apolitical society. Ganesh is not a political leader though he has the natural talent for it. His society is not politically conscious though it is alert and aggressive when it feels threatened; group action is natural. Neither leaders nor voters are at all aware of the outside world as a challenge to them or as judging them. Politics is not part of the social consciousness of his country--the public votes for personalities not for issues.

Ganesh didn't have time for the affairs of the Hindu Association. The island elections were two months off and he found himself embroiled. Indarsingh had decided to go up in Ganesh's ward and it was this rather than the promptings of the Association or Beharry or Swami that made Ganesh stand for the elections.(193)

We held no election meetings, but Swami and Partap arranged many prayer meetings for him. . . . Quite casually, in the middle of a lecture, he would say in Hindi, 'It may interest one or two of you in this gathering tonight to hear that I am a candidate for the elections next month. I can promise nothing. In everything I shall consult God and my conscience even at the risk of displeasing you. (194)

Ganesh's election committee arranges a Bhagwat and a free lunch and invites Indarsingh to it.

Indarsingh came in an Oxford blazer and Swami, as organiser of the *Bhagwat*, introduced him to the audience. 'I got to talk English to introduce this man to you, because I don't think he could talk any Hindi. . . . Ladies and gentlemen--Mr. Indarsingh, Bachelor of Arts of Oxford University, London, England.'

Indarsingh gave a little hop, fingered his tie, and, stupidly, talked about politics.

Indarsingh lost his deposit and had a big argument with the secretary of the PPU who had also lost his. Indarsingh said that the PPU had promised to compensate members who lost

62

their deposits. He found he was talking to nobody; for after the election results the Party for Progress and Unity just disappeared. (194)

Though only twenty pages describe Ganesh's actual entry into politics the whole book moves towards it by describing him in various roles which involve awareness of the public.

Here it might be well to pause awhile and consider the circumstances of Ganesh's rise, from teacher to masseur, from masseur to mystic, from mystic to M.L.C. In his autobiography, *The Years of Guilt*, which he began writing at this time, Ganesh attributes his success (he asks to be pardoned for using the word) to God.... If he had been born ten years earlier it is unlikely, if you take into account the Trinidad Indian's attitude to education at that time, that his father would have sent him to the Queen's Royal College. He might have become a pundit, and a mediocre pundit. If he had been born ten years later his father would have sent him to America or Canada or England to get a profession--the Indian attitude to education had changed so completely--and Ganesh might have become an unsuccessful lawyer or a dangerous doctor.... Nobody wants the quack dentist or the unqualified masseur in Trinidad now; and Ganesh's former colleagues of the world of massage have had to keep on driving taxis, but at three cents a mile now, so great is the competition. (199-200)

He can communicate successfully; he is aware of his environment; he has the ability to mould public opinion and to foresee failure, to move out in time. His final awakening to the possible meaning of politics is suppressed. It does not receive the necessary public support. He works out a new political theory with Indarsingh-Socialinduism. But

Just when he was going to show how the strike could be the

63

first step in establishing Socialinduism in Trinidad, the storm
broke. (211-12)

However

Indarsingh was elected in Ganesh's old ward, on a platform
of modified Socialinduism. (214)

The Mystic Masseur, in spite of its claims to objectivity, is a
subjective account of the island politician in the 1950s. The book
is also a 'tongue in cheek' comment on the concept of biographical
writing as a revelation of truth. For all his efforts to assemble
objective data about Ganesh (autobiographical material, eyewit-
ness accounts, newspaper reports, reported dialogue and conversation) the organizing sensibility touches it up with his own vision.

The Suffrage of Elvira is a dramatic account of the political
awakening of the village of Elvira--remote, unconnected and
dinghy. Its knowledge of the outside world is limited to the comings
and goings of the two American girls, Jehovah's witnesses, or the
frankly money-making activities of Mr. Surajpat Harbans, P.W.D.
contractor as well as proprietor of the transport company which
transports the road-building materials. It is during the election
campaign that it realizes the value of a printing press as a medium
of communication and coercion. The political losses and gains of
the members of this community can be literally assessed in unam-
biguous material terms. The literal personality of this village is
established and summed up by the narrator in the Prologue and the
Epilogue. Elvira is "the smallest, most isolated and most neglected
of the nine counties of Trinidad." (9) And it has not changed
significantly as a consequence of the elections:

So, Harbans won the election and the insurance company lost
a Jaguar. Chittaranjan lost a son-in-law and Dhaniram lost a
daughter-in-law. Elvira lost Lorkhoor and Lorkhoor won a
reputation. Elvira lost Mr. Cuffy. And Preacher lost his
deposit. (207)

Elvira, like Miguel Street, has a public personality. Its striking feature is the cohesiveness of its inhabitants in spite of the conflicts of race, religion and personal interests. They live very much in the present propelled by immediate needs. They can put aside their differences to unite in the demand for cases of whiskey for the whole community or for a religious thanksgiving ceremony for the victory of Harbans: they can recognise justice when they see it and can speak as one voice in their claim for fair play. Those who want to get away are few--Lorkhoor, Dulahin, Teacher Francis, Nelly--but they have no goals--just a feeling of being deprived by staying on in Elvira. Harbans and Chittaranjan are the truly trapped. Harbans has invested so much money to win this election that he cannot escape Elvira even though he privately disowns her. He feels less welcome than Tiger, the mongrel pup, among those who courted him before the elections. The fact of his mobility and residence in Port of Spain, providing an immediate escape from Elvira, diminishes his existential despair at his heavy losses:

Harbans was talking to the back of his hands. 'New symbol, eh? New slogan. New posters. What sin I do to get myself in this big big mess in my old old age?' (146)

When Harbans was leaving Elvira he was stopped by Mahadeo, and lacked spirit even to make his little joke: 'How much Hindu sick today? And what-and-what is the various entrance fee?' Mahadeo offered his list sadly and received the entrance fees a little more sadly.

When Harbans had left Elvira and was in County Caroni, he stopped the lorry and shook his small fist at the dark countryside behind him. 'Elvira!' he shouted. 'You is a bitch! A bitch! A bitch!' (147)

Chittaranjan knows that the chances of getting Harbans's son for a son-in-law are doubtful, he yet tries and his loss in money and aim is no surprise to him. He has to live with the knowledge of failure. But his campaigning for the elections on behalf of Harbans has democratized his existence. Nelly has been allowed to go to

65

England for further studies. And the village aristocrat has finally made friends with his disreputable neighbour and lifelong enemy-- Ramlogan, the rum shop owner.

> Ramlogan ran with the fruit to the back room and then followed Mrs. Chittaranjan out of the shop.
> Chittaranjan was leaning on the wall of his veranda.
> Ramlogan shouted, 'Hello, brothers!'
> Chittaranjan waved and widened his smile. 'You all right, brothers?'
> 'Yes, brothers. She bring the breadfruit and the zaboca for me. Ripe zaboca too, brothers.'
> 'They did look ripe to me too.'
> Ramlogan was near the wire fence. He hesitated.
> 'Is all right, brothers,' Chittaranjan said.
> 'Is much your fence as mine.'
> 'Nice fence, brothers.' (140)
> And so democracy took root in Elvira. (193)

The third person omniscient narrator develops the predilection campaign farcically only to bring Harbans to the tragic sense of being betrayed which, superseding his persistent knowledge of himself as betrayer, leaves him for a moment helpless and defeated unable to articulate his puzzlement:

> And then Harbans knew. No one in Elvira was fighting for him. All Elvira--Preacher, Lorkhoor, Baksh, Chittaranjan, Dhaniram and everybody else--all of them were fighting him.
> He was nearly seized with another fit of pessimism. . . . Then he thought of the sign he had had: the white women and the stalled engine, the black bitch and stalled engine. He had seen what the first meant. The women had stalled him in Cordoba.
> But the dog. What about the dog? Where was that going to stall him? (53)

The stray black bitch on account of whom Harbans's lorry stalls in its uphill climb to Elvira, as a premonition of disaster, assumes the literary proportions of the bitch which Elvira becomes and of Fate itself. So superstition defines politics as a personal engagement with Fate, as Ganesh is never tired of saying. And like Ganesh, Harbans is sure of winning for he feels he is one of the elect:

> But deep down, despite everything, he knew he was going to win. He cried and raged; but he wanted to fool, not tempt, fate. (53)

This self-confidence, generated out of a single-minded self-devotion makes him blind to the picaroon nature of the society of which he is a member. He does not see himself as they see him--an exploitable resource, not a human being. This mutual blindness, arising out of urgent unfulfilled needs, creates the dramatic tension in the novel.

The narrator's omniscience equips him to round out the several characters as individual consciousness of the village capable of solidarity even in dissent. Their mutual dependence is an awareness of the closed and enclosing nature of their existence which expands into all forms of alienation from the life of the rest of the country: economic, social, psychological and philosophical. Life here is lived at subsistence level.

What sets Harbáns apart from the group with whom he is working closely and whose interests he seeks to represent in the government is his greater imaginative self-involvement so that the external contexts of politics and money become indexes to individuality. He has more money than he knows what to do with yet money is his motive for entering politics. The dyspeptic, anxious, timid, lonely Harbans (his wife never enters the scene and his son is a political convenience) knocks one of the witnesses off her bike as his lorry stalls while climbing Elvira Hill. He is concerned first for himself.

'Fust time it happen,' Harbans said, almost in a whisper. 'Fust time in more than twenty years.' (10)

The woman tries to convince him not to be worried as she is not hurt, not realizing that his thoughts are far from her condition:

'Eh?' he said to his hands, and paused. 'Eh? All right?' He paused again. 'You sure?' (10)

Money being a concrete reality, unable to expand like a metaphor, Harbans is the loser of what he prizes most and for which he is courted by the villagers. He realizes he has been outwitted:

Harbans spent the rest of that night settling his bills. The taxi-drivers had to be paid off, Ramlogan's rum-account settled, petrol vouchers honoured, agents given bonuses. And when all that was done, Harbans left Elvira, intending never to return. (194)

Elvira, as the antagonist, becomes the existential knowledge of the other as enemy. And so a simple concrete situation evolves into dangerous existential despair as the narrator plays with the minimal counters of exchange that circulate as the sense of human understanding in the village: money, food, drink, possessions, sickness, death and parental responsibility are all subsumed under the general superstitious self-centred attitude to life. This apprehension of the other as resistant to the self is a recurring experience for Naipaul's protagonists. The other is articulated as the enemy who cannot be located and destroyed. Helpless, the protagonist is forced to come to terms with it. In "One Out of Many" Santosh marries the hubshi, the embodiment of all that is to be feared as a despoiler of the self. The narrator of "Tell Me Who to Kill" retreats into a subjective world of fantasy as an escape from the hostile world which has alienated his brother, in whom he has invested his identity, from him. Singh in *The Mimic Men* analyses his insincerity as the result of his inability to 'kill the enemy' when he gets the chance to do so.

The ironic/satiric tone of the narrator makes him an indirect participant, an observer, in the drama of Elvira. He speaks like an insider become an outsider. He dramatizes the chronological sequence of events of the period preceding the elections and reserves his comments for the epilogue and prologue. He shows the development of democracy in a vacuum which makes a mimicry of the whole concept of community and individual responsibility. The minimum terms of survival being economic material self-interest rather than any platform of political action activates the various alliances. These alliances change partners as rapidly as in a country dance guided by the desire of extracting as much benefit from Harbans as is possible: medical welfare, burial expenses, free drinks at Cuffy's wake and to celebrate victory, vans, loudspeakers, marriage alliances and business deals. The other factor which stresses their literal existence and guides their votes is their preconceived notions: the fear of magic and obeah in the shape of the unsuspecting Tiger as the sign of evil things to come. The presence of Tiger releases similar older memories of dreams and signs in other residents of the village and altogether helps to build up the prevailing sinister atmosphere intensified by the sudden death of Cuffy and the disappearance of Dulahin. So that, for the older generation, democracy and the gift of the vote becomes a symptom of bad times. As Mrs. Baksh says:

'Who fault it is that this whole thing happen?' Her brow darkened and her manner changed. 'Is this election sweetness that sweeten you up, Baksh. But see how this sweetness going to turn sour sour. See.'
She was righter than she knew. (82)

The younger generation is as entrapped as their elders but they are aware of it and hate it and wish to get away from it. As individuals they might escape their physical and economic deprivation. But the lack of educational opportunities or the mimic nature of those available has entrapped them in repetitive patterns of behaviour though the elections have brought the promise of a wider

69

world.

> But while he drove about Central Trinidad in his loudspeaker
> van, speaking faultless English to his heart's content, Foam
> had to remain in Elvira, an apprentice in his father's shop.
> Foam hated the stuffy dark shop, hated the eternal tacking,
> which was all he was allowed to do, hated Elvira, at moments
> almost hated his family. (39-40)

Foam summarizes the younger generation's greater awareness of
political reality as a process of maturation:

> 'You shy, Mr. Harbans,' Foam said. 'I know how it is. But
> you going to get use to this waving. Ten to one, before this
> election over, we going to see you waving and shouting to
> everybody, even to people who ain't going to vote for you.'
>   Harbans shook his head sadly.
>   Foam settled into the angle of the seat and the door. 'Way
> I see it is this. In Trinidad this democracy is a brand new thing.
> We is still creeping. We is a creeping nation.' He dropped his
> voice solemnly: 'I respect people like you, you know, Mr.
> Harbans, doing this thing for the first time.' (25)

For Harbans and Ganesh politics has meant success of a kind
which had absorbed their sense of failure. Ganesh as M.B.E. can
forget his political defeat by Indar Singh. Harbans is only temporarily non-plussed. He can still look forward to financial gains
which will banish the pain of his losses. Imaginative, idealistic,
romantic Ralph Ranjeet Kirpal Singh, hero of the autobiography
The Mimic Men, playing the game of politics on a larger scale,
unable to compromise or withdraw, is forced to leave the country
in disgrace. Deprived of all social standards of success (wife, home,
money, friends, status, leadership and children) he experiences a
loss of aspiration. His failure as politician signifies to him the
failure of Trinidad to be a nation. Hence the autobiography has a
political focus.

His Isabellan background is essentially the same as that of Harbans and Ganesh only more complex. Born and brought up in the urban culture of the capital, with roots neither in land nor money nor a tradition of achievement he has a more immediate contact with Western culture. This unreal reality only encourages him to reject the 'ordinariness' of his island life and to seek for the golden landscapes described in English books and by nostalgic expatriate British teachers. His own overactive imaginative life colours and modifies his awareness of actually compounding his errors and agonies. Much later, on reflection, he bitterly expresses the mimic nature of his life and personality in words which have the overtones of a political awareness.

> There, in Liege in a traffic jam, on the snow slopes of the Laurentians, was the true, pure world. We, here on our island, handling books printed in this world, and using its goods, had been abandoned and forgotten. We pretended to be real, to be learning, to be preparing ourselves for life, we mimic men of the New World, one unknown corner of it, with all its reminders of the corruption that came so quickly to the new. (146)

Nevertheless political failure and humiliation at home and abroad, exile in London coming at the end of devastating personal failures each pressing down on his sense of non-existence becomes for Singh the impetus of a life which will deny this death.

> The occasions that followed are a blur: of encounters less with individual bodies than with anonymous flesh. Each occasion pressed me deeper down into emptiness, that prolonged sensation of shock with which I was every minute of every day trying to come to terms. (28)

Such was the exile of Mr. Mural's witness; and dignity and aloofness implied an audience. It wasn't like this: a man sitting at the limit of desolation with sixty-six pounds of luggage in two Antler suitcases, concentrating on the moment, which he must not relate to anything else. And who will later give me even Mr. Mural's proof of this moment? It was a moment of total helplessness. It occurred on an afternoon of sunshine, while the holiday trains passed.

That was a long time ago. Such a moment cannot return. . . . An absurd moment, but from it and by it I measure my recovery *Je vens d' lué.* (250)

He turns to writing as an assertion of existence. It is the only means of survival; for in politics he has exhausted the scope of the 'good' life. Politics, as the widest and most comprehensive sphere of his active life becomes the parameter of his narrative. It defines the terms of his understanding of himself and his society. He sees both as driftwood cast up on remote island shores because they are unable to impress their existence on the sophisticated political consciousness of the West. Singh recounts his visit as minister leading the government delegation to London to renegotiate the bauxite contract. His arrogant dismissal by his counterpart in London hurts all the more for he recognizes him as an inferior man:

> It was a brief, humiliating meeting. This man, whom in other, humbler capacities I had met more than once before on various government trips to London and had thought affable and slightly foolish, now barely had time for the courtesies. His manner indicated clearly that our game had gone on long enough and he had other things to do than to assist the public relations of colonial politicians. In about forty-five seconds he painted so lively a picture of the consequences of any intemperate action by the government of Isabella that I felt personally rebuked. (244)

He discerns the same studied arrogance and diplomatic flippancy in Lord Stockwell's attitude to his serious wish to discuss the labour problem of the former's sugar estate in Isabella. Lord Stockwell prefers to comment on his rich hair and talk about his visit with Singh's father, the Gurudev, who having wisely given up politics

72

has relevantly made his life a spiritual mission. This disparity between his own sense of importance of his mission and its casual dismissal by these representatives of power and democracy makes Singh sick to the soul and he indulges in further masochistic exercises in nullity pandering to Stella and deliberately seeking an encounter with a prostitute on an unnamed island stopover on his return journey to Isabella. But his successive alienation also defines his individual purpose to move on even if the direction is not clear. His dream is suggestive:

> I had not slept well. In a serial dream I had found myself on my back, on my belly, in a London street or tunnel through which red underground trains careered on crisscrossing tracks. Beyond the trains I could see Sally, Sandra, My father, Lord Stockwell, anxious to come to me, who could not move towards them. As I slept and awakened, waiting for the light to come to the fantasy city, known and unknown, memory and the dream flowed together. When the light came I was weak and ill. The stopover was at an end. It was necessary to rise and prepare for another departure. (237-38)

Political awakening, as a sense of historical time and place, comes with political humiliation. But it is more than the knowledge of the politics of power, of success and failure. Lord Stockwell's sophisticated diplomacy has brought home to him his links with Trinidad--its colonial history--its inexperience and innocence being the reason for its unimportance and isolation. There is no escape from his past and no future outside it.

> To be born on an island like Isabella, an obscure New World transplantation, second-hand and barbarous, was to be born to disorder.... Now I was to discover that disorder has its own logic and permanence: the Greek was wise. Even as I was formulating my resolve to escape, there began that series of events which, while sharpening my desire to get away, yet rooted me more firmly to the locality where accident had

placed me. (118)

R.R.K. Singh, living an anonymous life in London, turns to narration as a means of the final emptying out of the past self in order to start a new life afresh--to take up the challenge of the west. Ironically enough, he does so along the older known pattern of experience. He hopes for financial uplift, possibly regular employment if his book gets published but most of all "to find himself the object of an awe which he will not of course acknowledge."

> It never occurred to me that the writing of this book might have become an end in itself, that the recording of a life might become an extension of that life. (244)

However writing becomes an experience bridging the historical gap between his Aryan ancestors and the modern East Indian West Indian sensibility gripped by the existential anguish of alienation, homelessness, rootlessness which devours contemporary political sensibility all over the world, seeking its final resting place in the world of matter, reason, logic and imagination. The horseman leader of Aryan hordes sees his vision partially fulfilled in himself as the Aryan householder turning to meditation.

For the narrator Trinidad remains a time-bound personal metaphor unable to provide the creative impulse for being--the poetic vision--though he has wrested from it his possibility of survival. His personal and political positive experiences remain unlinked with his major knowledge of disaster, self-disgust, dandyism (negative self-knowledge). His tender moments with Sally and his genuine compassion for the sufferings of his countrymen (recalling the child's pity for the labourers which he feels has been the sincere ground for political passion in the Third World) remain as incidents that are recalled to be left along the wayside of his narrative journey. Though they provide the dialectical impulse of his life restraining total annihilation, this knowledge never comes to his consciousness to act as a force binding the account into a novel.

Singh's political theorizing, arising out of his experience, is purely descriptive.[11] He draws out the connections between the childhood and adult life of a politician to reveal the accidental nature of island politics. The island politician is a born leader of men who finds himself in politics as a matter of chance rather than choice. Singh enters politics as an antidote to a broken marriage, because it is the 'thing to do' for a man of his status and qualifications and because he is 'egged on' by his friend Browne. Ganesh was similarly urged by Leila and the Great Belcher. The concept of politics as a theory of government and nationhood and integrity of character and action is absent. The questing and questioning of reality and experience, the ability to turn actuality into an area of speculation, to move beyond it to the formulation of principles and policies, to the subtleties of thought and expression which characterizes the life of the 'secure,' remain outside the narrative vision of Singh. Unlike Stella, he would not have been able to convey his desires through a discussion of nursery rhymes and children's books or an important refusal as courteously as Lord Stockwell did. Though Singh does hint at his awareness of the larger world by saying that the conservation at the Lord Stockwell's dinner party was being conducted in 'an unfamiliar mode,' it is Naipaul who makes available to the reader the larger political reality as the dialectic between the novel *The Mimic Men* and the untitled narrative without an identifiable genre which Singh writes.

The convoluted style of the highly self-conscious literary biography that Singh writes suggests the narrator's belief in politics as a historical process in which man, moment and place all have to be accounted for. The politician, to be known must be studied 'en situation.' Negation of physical life as the mood of the novel is built up by the protagonist's resistance to restructuring it on more satisfactory lines, for alternatives in his society are missing and to this is added the emotional destruction caused by a too literal society on a sensitive mind:

I know that return to my island and to my political life is impossible. The pace of colonial events is quick, the turnover of leaders rapid. I have already been forgotten; and I know that the people who supplanted me are themselves about to be supplanted. My career is by no means unusual. It falls into the pattern. The career of the colonial politician is short and ends brutally. We lack order. Above all, we lack power, and we do not understand that we lack power. We mistake words and the acclamation of words for power; as soon as our bluff is called we are lost. Politics for us are a do-or-die, once-for-all charge. Once we are committed we fight more than political battles: we often fight quite literally for our lives. Our transitional or make-shift societies do not cushion us. There are no universities or city houses to refresh us and absorb us after the heat of battle. For those who lose, and nearly everyone in the end loses, there is only one course: flight. Flight to the greater disorder, the final emptiness: London and the home counties.[12]

The pattern of his life is characterized by homelessness (personal and political). He is unable to create a home, for all memories of home have turned to nothing. His childhood home was a boarding house, so emotionally unsatisfactory was his life in it. His home with Sandra remained childless and the marriage broke up. He sees the Roman House, an unreal order he has imposed on his society and himself, as the cause of his political failure--his imagination working on the borders of superstition and reason. His final retreat into the faceless boarding house in London also permits him his maximum freedom, committed only to himself and the moment. No more challenges for him.

As the narration develops the reader sees the protagonist unable to move out of his context, physical and mental. He remains the 'island innocent' who chooses existential sincerity to political/materialistic sophistication. But he succeeds in evolving a pattern of authentic life which grants him a sense of freedom and wholeness within his context as he accepts himself as he is, trying to understand but not trying to become the other.

Naipaul has presented Singh as a consciousness which is

76

more evolved than that of Ganesh or Harbans. Natural ability and sensibility, a natural empathetic awareness of the other combined with unrelenting pursuit of the truth of the self, charts out a course of development which seemingly haphazard, is all along a matter of choice and will, guided by conscious self-reflection. His political exile becomes the furthest extreme of objective life from which life only as inward movement is possible. The same pursuit of truth of the self which made him the dandy and which pushed him into politics now carries him to the other extreme of complete self-negation. The act of writing is a recovery of balance. Trinidad, always the antagonist, the measure of his failure in life, becomes the measure of his success as an individual and as a writer.

The three novels together discuss the relationship between political and personal anonymity in a situation in which the individual is yet unable to distinguish his individuality apart from that of his society. So that the apolitical society and the 'island politician' are equivalent terms for non-existence through alienation from the contemporary world of power politics. Politics, apart from tourism, is the only situation available to Trinidad within which to communicate with the rest of the world. Hence political non-existence acquires the same significance as the extreme situation from which recovery becomes impossible for the anti-hero of Krieger's *The Tragic Vision;* Kurtz of *Heart of Darkness* is the prototype.

The personal and social correlation defines the subjective/objective dialectic in the novels. Naipaul depicts political confusion and corruption as analogous to the personal confusion and corruption which lies beneath the even surface of social conformity. Simultaneously the political situation reveals the growing alienation between protagonist and society. The narrator/protagonist of *The Mystic Masseur* directs his irony at Ganesh as an approved representative of his society. Harbans is similarly aware of a gap between his society and himself which is not further explored by the narrator, for the purpose of the novel is to present democracy in practice. R.R.K. Singh, at the age of forty, realizes that though his political career in Isabella has ended, life as a writer offers a different kind of satisfaction. Writing requires anonymity as privacy; and so he embraces willingly the condition that he sought to escape when he left Isabella as a student and which was forced upon him in his political failure.

The three novels dwell on the absurdities of democracy as a form of government which has not evolved out of the needs of the people.[13] At best democratic government in the country of its birth is an uneasy marriage between capitalism and democracy where the interests of the moneyed classes prevail. In Trinidad it has unleashed the avaricious instincts of a society which is already picaroon. Naipaul in presenting Trinidad 'en situation' suggests that democracy reveals its state of being adrift completely. Politics is the challenge as well as the trap for the Trinidadian consciousness. He necessarily understands the meaning of political freedom in terms of the colonial definition: in the framework in which it was handed over to him--democracy as the rage for power to be attained through money as the medium of exchange which purchases all requirements. It awakens the Trinidadian to the knowledge of undiscovered areas which need exploring though the goal is visible. It will enable him to speak with dignity and possess in identity; he will be equal with the rest of the world. However, not having a political past politics does not form part of the composite ideal consciousness of the individual. It alienates him from his past without providing him with a supporting environment, leaving him suspended. Lacking sophistication and power Trinidad and other third world countries continue to be used as political stooges in the larger game of the bigger powers, who along with arms export their culture in the holds of gunboats.[14]

In these novels Naipaul has underlined the conditions of world communication as being essentially political in nature; Trinidad's unpreparedness to do so at that level is its failure. Political anxiety has introduced the dialogue between the person and his nation but political awareness is necessary before it can communicate with the rest of the world.

Political reality structurally represents the multivalent poetic vision in these novels. The political situation in Trinidad reflects microcosmically the larger political disparities: highlighting the community of need disguised by ideologies. It speaks the universal language of corruption and the prostitution of politics. Politics controls material existence and so political manouvering becomes the minimum condition of world survival. Naipaul presents two antithetic political situations--one objectively and the other subjectively, camouflaged by a superficial, deceptive resemblance which masquerades as democracy, independence and equality. One is powerful, secure, superior and patronizing. The other is weak, insecure and obsessed by a sense of unimportance. Both, egotistical and unscrupulous, meet under the mantle of democratically free nations. Trinidad's lack of historical perspective makes it absurd. It accepts unhesitatingly its newly imposed identity as it accepted its colonial and slave status in the past. It thinks seriously of jumping across time and place, of disregarding the facts of its material/historical reality, to reach out to possibilities which become escapist fantasies or mimic realities.

Political reality as the setting which regulates the structure of his novels enables Naipaul to present a fresh perspective on the function of time and place in the novel. In the Western novel chronological time assumes a secure world. A chronological time asserts the superiority of the individual over the material world. Superiority and security characterize the cynics, clowns, fools, Lears and Wandering Jews of the Western novel. They, like Stella or Jane, can discuss and reveal and indulge themselves and their agonies, play the role of the homeless, for they have a place to run back to. Cordelia will take care of her mad father. Both divisions of time create formulas of timeless, placeless worlds which are as secure and permanent as eternity. Both elevate Western man to the necessary and the ideal. Naipaul is able to establish by contrast the vulnerability which thrusts a man and a nation further into an existing alienation and hence anonymity. Naipaul's narrator, subverting the chronological and objective order he has created through subjective ordering of his protagonist's life and by questioning that order in his tone of irony and satire, creates the terror of placelessness and timelessness as a void--a pit without a bottom.

The clock as an organizer of natural time, and as awareness of the contemporary material world, caters to the sense of man's sameness the world over. Paradoxically, Naipaul points out that in practice chronological time means different things in different places. Place, being a reality available to the senses, is a universal experience. Its impact cannot be denied or overlooked. Continuity of experience is assured through continuous change of place. Hence a 'sense of place,' as a poignant awareness of reality, can reorder man's inherited time sense to establish a rhythm of understanding which alone makes communication effective and possible. Political reality, as the 'sense of place' is then a proportionate understanding of self and Trinidad in relation to the national and international community.

NOTES

1. V.S. Naipaul, *The Middle Passage* (Harmondsworth: Penguin, 1978), p. 78.

2. V.S. Naipaul, *The Mimic Men* (Harmondsworth: Penguin, 1977), p. 208.

3. Cf. "Novelists of the Colonial Experience," *The Colonial Encounter*, M.M. Mahmood (London: Rex Collings, 1977).

4. V.S. Naipaul, *The Loss of El Dorado* (Hamondsworth: Penguin, 1973), p. 332.

5. Cf. Thomas L. Hartshorne, "From 'Catch-22' To 'Slaughterhouse-V,'" *The American Review*, Vol. 26, no.1, 1981, pp. 9-20. Garrett Epps, "Politics as Metaphor," *The American Review*, vol. 26, no. 1, 1981, pp. 21-35.

6. *The Mimic Men*, p. 206.

7. V.S. Naipaul, *The Mystic Masseur* (London: Andre Deutsch, 1957), p. 8.

8. V.S. Naipaul, *The Suffrage of Elvira* (Harmondsworth: Penguin, 1981), p. 9.

9. *Ibid.*, p. 11.

10. *The Mimic Men*, pp. 98-9.
11. Cf. See also M.M. Mahmood, "The Dispossessed," *The Colonial Encounter.*
12. *The Mimic Men*, p. 8.
13. Cf. Harold J. Laski, *A Grammar of Politics*, 4th edition (London: George Allen and Unwin, 1955), p. 2.

    "No theory of the State is ever intelligible save in the context of its time. What men think about the state is the outcome always of the experience in which they are immersed."

    "Our age, in this regard, is no different from its predecessors. It is an age of critical transition in which, as at the end of the fifteenth and the eighteenth centuries, a new social order is struggling grimly to be born. Our scheme of values is in the melting pot, and the principles of its refashioning have not yet been determined. As always, in such a time, men have to explain the foundations of politics, and they seek anew to explain the nature and functions of the state."
14. Cf. Robin Mathews, *Canadian Literature: Surrender or Revolution*, ed. Gail Dexter (Toronto: Steel Rail Educational Publishing, 1978), p. 4.

    Robin Mathews, in his essay "Literature and Colonialism" analyses this state in his country as the consequence of the 'staples economy' practised by the Canadian operating class in collaboration with the U.S.A.: "The operating class has not been interested in making Canada a genuine home, the place of primary significance."

Social Reality and its Caveat:
A House for Mr. Biswas;
Mr. Stone and the Knights Companion

In *The Mystic Masseur*, *The Suffrage of Elvira* and *The Mimic Men*, the political situation of Trinidad emerges as an aspect of the larger social reality of the protagonist. It expresses his natural optimistic awareness of the larger world both as his historico-existential landscape and as the widest definition of material reality. He is a man who arrives at the marginal apprehension of the notion: ''The modern world, after all, cannot be caricatured or conjured away; a pastoral past cannot be reestablished.''¹ For the narrator the political actions of his protagonists provide unassailable objective grounds for exposing them as human beings conditioned by a historical environment and so to establish a rationale for Trinidad's alienation and insignificance in the power-oriented political world. The narrator's polyvalent tone--sympathetic, satiric, ironic--indicating his overt alienation yet subconscious identification, establishes his dual vision of the protagonist as an individual and as a member of a community. Naipaul exploits his protagonist and narrator to depict socio/political alienation in the contemporary world: nations surviving frantically in mutual exclusiveness. Political reality in these novels emerges as a ground for cold war rather than mutual cooperation.

In *A House for Mr. Biswas* and *Mr. Stone and the Knights Companion* the immediate societies of the protagonists, Mohun Biswas and Richard Stone, have smothered their natural sense of the larger social reality instead of providing a passage to it. This social reality, which surfaces in their fantasies, indicates its hidden presence as the need for a vision of the self. Mohun Biswas identifies his highest achievement with owning a house. Stone's vision is a desire to penetrate to the truth of the relationship between the corruptible, finite body and the infinite, pure world of ideas. So the protagonists of these novels, alienated from their societies and their social realities, are seen to move without a sense of direction. Paradoxically, the standards of their respective societies are also the limits of their individual horizons.

The two novels vary widely in geographical location and in portrayal of character and society. One is set in rural South Trinidad, warm, humid and fertile with its city life only an extension of rural culture. London is cosmopolitan and industrial, dark and cold, with nature converted into an artifact of city life. The historical period is roughly the same. (The two taken together would illustrate what Naipaul means by 'sense of place.' In the same historical period it is hard to imagine two such widely differing societies existing simultaneously. A modem sensibility would need to be aware of the differences that exist in the world in order to appreciate it truly as a human society of unequals).[1] Though the protagonist in each case is the Prufrockian man Biswas's existential struggles bear no resemblance to those of Stone. Biswas's life is a series of minor disasters, each of which can be seen as his angry rebuttal of an uncongenial society which exhausts him in early middle age. And his final peace is as much a consequence of a personal triumph as of exhaustion, sickness and failure rationalized and accepted. Stone's life, after an early harrowing experience of loss and pain, proceeds evenly, surrounded by a tomb-like peace. The three years of his life recorded in the novel are an account of the upheaval which destroys this peace and his recovery of it at a different level. It also has the same new quality of patience which characterizes Biswas's waiting for life to wear itself out.

Yet in the mood of despair at 'imminent extinction' which is the crucial experience of each protagonist the inability of contemporary society to make life meaningful for its most ordinary members becomes apparent. Society's basic orientation to the past

makes it resistant to the individual's existential needs and awarenesses. The opposition in these novels is not only between the
marginal man and his society, but also between society and the
larger social reality. The former is presented by the narrator as a too
literal static situation which prevents an individual from breaking
through to a society based on mutual understanding and appreciation rather than on needs created by that particular society. Man is
the victim of his society rather than its guide and beneficiary. Social
reality keeps man in step with his times. But any society which
encourages and engenders dependency--a desire for security rather
than creativity and equality--and is coercive, necessarily utilizes the
past as a weapon of control, hampering its members from moving
into the present: it is an inadequate society.›

In the widely different settings of these two novels Naipaul is
able to suggest a fluid social reality beyond the level at which
societies function which is the ground for human agreement. The
obviously different narrators are affected by a similar mood and
probe for its causes beyond their apparent sources in the contemporary situation of each protagonist to a more fundamental understanding of human responses to existence and nonexistence. It is
possible for Naipaul and the narrator to realize this relationship
between the individual and society, society and social reality, the
particular and the universal, past and present, at different levels of
consciousness because of their respective understanding of man's
relationship to his environment.

The boundary that separates an individual's consciousness
from the consciousness of the society in which he lives, unlike
political reality, is relatively fluid. The distinction between subjective and objective cannot be as clearly defined for the interaction
between the two is not always visible or known. The narrator can
depend on the concreteness of political action to reveal totally the
individual and social preoccupations of the protagonist. It represents, in the context of those novels projecting the political reality
of Trinidad, the conjunction and conflation of the subjective and the
objective. Society is more apt to become a part of the individual's
mental landscape and vice versa and is by its nature restrictive. The

84

values generated by this relationship are subject to fluctuation and are not supportive, giving way under the pressure of a crisis. Biswas's emotional comprehension of the Tulsi house alters rapidly depending on whether he feels the need for security or desires freedom from restraint! The knowledge of Tulsi security is also his experience of existential suffocation. A promise as well as a threat, its ambivalent nature is insufficient to combat the existential fear of extinction which leads to his nervous breakdown. Mr. Stone's understanding of Margaret varies according to the situation which gives rise to his reflection on her. At times she appears dowdy and at other times she is charming and feminine. His vision of his society is often coloured by hers and at other times she is the antagonist to be escaped.

To draw a consistent picture of this narrow society the narrator projects it through the jaundiced eyes of the protagonist, who responds to it by trying to set up an unconventional existence. One is simultaneously aware of the narrator's satiric/ironic tone directed at the protagonist as a representative of his society; he finally succumbs to society's conventional role-playing demands. Stone's alienation from his environment is a response of withdrawal from a situation he cannot cope with. Biswas's alienation is the consequence of his vivid imaginative life created and sustained by the alien influences of his education and his reading which channelize his ambitions unrealistically. Both men, though sensitive, imaginative and, to a degree, rational, are not thinkers and planners who exercise conscious control over the direction of their lives. They are unable to transcend the limitations of which they are conscious.

Naipaul operates the dialectical pattern of the novel through the differing consciousnesses of the protagonist and the narrator both responding to the same narrow external reality and so, indirectly, to each other. He thus suggests the complexity of the relationship between man and his historical environment and his inability to escape it. He can rise above it momentarily, like Mr. Stone in his moving chair defying gravity, to a more universal philosophical apprehension of his dilemma. Like Biswas, he can realize that one's portion of the earth is all a lucky man can hope to possess after a lifetime of endeavour. Both acquire a new humility by a ready and gracious acceptance of actual life--which is an urgent awareness of the perishable nature of one's body as the only source of the self. The narrator's transcendence through his dual vision of distance and identification does not suggest a release from his society. Narration for him is a more coherent form of the life of fantasy that Biswas and Stone indulge in to escape material restraints. He is unable to suggest a new direction or alternative to his present society.

The social reality in these two divergent novels, sagas of reentry into society of the outsider, is confined to the immediate society, past and present, of Stone and Biswas. They converge in their portrayal of the stasis induced by contemporary society. Alienation becomes a condition of survival and is projected in the novels as the fantasies of free movement that the protagonists indulge in to relieve depression and boredom. A very restricted world, geographically and aesthetically, it is extended by a journey, literal and metaphorical, undertaken by the protagonist. This journey enables him to view his past in perspective releasing him from it and from his pre-formed notions of himself. His movement away from his immediate environment becomes the condition for a breakthrough into the larger world and also his subsequent self-imprisonment.[4]

For the narrator the narrative is the journey which, as Ralph Singh says, adds the fourth dimension to his personality by becoming the vehicle of understanding, order and rehabilitation. He has distanced himself from his society and is able to present it as an outsider. The irony inherent in the titles of the novels acquires force when placed against the lengthy, egotistical involvements of the protagonist and the narrator. They yield a vision of a larger surrounding world to which they are not alive, a whole past tradition out of which these societies have evolved and which now has only ritual value and impresses the continuing need for shelter and companionship. The freedom and security each secures becomes questionable as it is gained by turning their backs to the world and to the future: to place and to time. They fail to engage intellectually with their society, to see it as a dialectical historical reality. The narrator, an outsider, presents a closed world, for effective consciousness of another society is absent in the novels. Their most positive orientation to their social reality is expressed by a desire for accommodation within their respective societies. The reader sees the journey as a marginal movement away from an original position which is subjectively fulfilling but does not manifest sufficient opposition to alter the direction of society.

Mr. Biswas, with his family and furniture, accumulating both in a haphazard fashion, moves through various Tulsi houses in the areas surrounding Arwacas, with Hanuman House as a frequent transfer point. His decisive journey to Port of Spain from Hanuman House after his recovery from the Greenvale disaster becomes a fresh start to a more successful life. He will not allow fear of failure, fear of Tulsi mockery, to immobilize him. His aesthetic development is naturally limited by his economic and social handicaps. But though his sensitivity to his environment and his imaginative capacity to identify with heroic characters in books is a major cause of his problems, these qualities also enable him to strive for aesthetic fulness in his daily life thus helping him to overcome his fear of death and his desire for continuity through Anand.

Mr. Stone's daily ritual and actual journey between his home and office varies only slightly to include the annual Christmas party at the Tomlinson residence and his annual winter vacations at his sister's houses as she moves from suburb to suburb of London. The uncharacteristic honeymoon trip to Cornwall destroys forever the induced peace of his patterned movements. Dislocated in unfamiliar surroundings, he achieves a new orientation to life so that all that was formerly excluded now enters into and forms part of his world. Margaret, the cat, the garden, Mrs. Millington, now become recipients of his love and sympathetic attention. And those he cannot accept, such as Whymper, Gwen and his neighbours--the whole world of values contrary to his own--are viewed with a condescending graciousness. His compulsive indulgence in fantasies of flying and overviewing private lives is toned down. He now reveals a more literary, verbal interest in life in his poetic reflections on man. Like Biswas his aesthetic consciousness centres on the appreciation of natural life.

The narrator's empathetic appraisal of the protagonist's predicament infiltrates the orthodox objective structure of the novel, rooted in organized concrete detail and chronology, setting in motion a static world. The strictly chronological order of narration, describing the incidents and episodes in the lives of the two protagonists, reflects the simple solidity of the societies in which they live. Its sense of chronology has seeped into the minds of the protagonists congealing the external world into a patterned existence. Their actions in it are not interactions with it and leave them hopelessly unanchored. Thus the actual movement of the novel is balanced by a certain sequential development of the protagonist's mind to maturity. The simple facts of their social life provide a strong contrast to their disorganized minds. Their efforts to extricate themselves from society's inhibiting simplicity and their own mental confusions provide the narrator with a concrete target for his satire and irony. Naipaul uses chronology as a peg which anchors in the actual situation of the protagonist, the narrator's polyvalent subjective journey so that the novel does not remain a reflection of his mind but develops dramatically. The hard facts of reality pulsate with a life which reduce the barbed attacks of the narrator to an exercise in intellectual word-play.

The third person omniscient narrator, focussing his vision on the manner in which the protagonist handles his society, directs his irony at the man and his society. He shows him as essentially incapable of meeting the demands of his times and so partially responsible for his imprisonment and alienation in his self-centred universe. He is a consequence as much of the restricting social structure as of his inability to use his imagination and sensibility effectively to release himself from it. He uses his abilities as escape mechanisms. For he is shown as deficient in the power to think constructively and creatively. It is the picture of a man unable to move outside his social context though he is aware of its inadequacy. The narrator presents the protagonist as a man who being at odds with his society is at odds with himself.

Both Stone and Biswas start life outside a context of meaningful human relationships which would involve them in the life of the community and so themselves become conveyors and modifiers of an active tradition. Their past is reported as a personal history without particular reference to it as an aspect of the history of their societies as in the case of the earlier novels studied. Besides this though the narrator's stance is objective we see society from the outsiders's points of view. We see the Tulsis as Biswas sees them: the destructive impregnability of Hanuman House dominating the novel to the end. Gwen and Whymper appear throughout at the subhuman, amoral and antisocial types that Stone categorizes them as being.

Stone and Biswas are marginal men from whom society as a stabilizing and sustaining experience was snatched away at an early age, almost fatalistically, leaving both orphans. An experience of freedom coupled with an excessive insecurity motivates their actions throughout the novels. Their lives become an almost propitiatory engagement with a hostile fate which society represents. They are not rebels against any social ideology. They are both law-abiding citizens. They do not break rules or indulge in antisocial practices for personal gain, as did the protagonists of the earlier-mentioned novels. An initial freedom makes them unfit, as egotists, to accommodation in social institutions which demand compromise. Yet their initial insecurity obsesses them with the desire for social security to the exclusion of all other possibilities inherent in it so that society becomes the final statement of propriety against which they measure themselves; society becomes a psychological metaphor for the self. Self-imprisoned, they value their subjective freedom as the attainment of a personal vision.

Alienation characterizes the relationship between the protagonist and the narrator. In spite of the latter's sympathy for the former they remain apart and both are outsiders to the society in which the former lives and which the latter describes. The narrator addresses his protagonists as Mr. Stone and Mr. Biswas; he never adopts the easy familiarity of tone with which he addresses the protagonists of *The Mystic Masseur*, *The Suffrage of Elvira* and *The Mimic Men* as Ganesh, Harbans and 'I' respectively.

The stilted orthodox tone on which each narrative ends reveals it as a fictional biography. The narrator, in each case, gives his own comic/philosophic interpretation of the protagonist's situation to round off the theme of non-existence. The latter's romantic vision bears the stamp of a cliché thought. Mr. Biswas's actual death becomes meaningful in terms of his life preceding it. He apprehends the life around him with the full force of his being. His house, his family, his furniture, his garden, all speak to him of the power of his manhood: the power to create, to possess and appreciate his own portion of earth. Mr. Biswas succeeds in leaving a mark which is fictionally evident only after his death. His house is empty without him but "it does not fall down." His non-being has created a temporary change in the environment. Similarly Stone meditates on his 'change of heart' as he walks home from the office one day when there is a transport strike. Now the tree in the yard and the new cat, the offspring of the old one which was destroyed, speak not only of the passing of time but of renewal. And so the fear of extinction is dissipated by the apprehension of continuity in nature. This positive expansion of consciousness becomes possible only through his forging of links with the environment by his marriage to Margaret. The narrators have developed these accounts as dialectics of physical and psychological being and non-being. The irony and parody grows out of their apprehension of the paradox of continuity realized in discontinuity of the physical self/in the loss of egotistical self-awareness.

Interaction between the narrator and the protagonist at a critical moment, as in the earlier group of novels, is noticeably absent. The crisis in these novels is described symbolically rather than dramatically. Thunder and heavy rain aggravate and project Biswas's neurotic fear of being destroyed when his half-built Greenvale house collapses. Mr. Stone's condition, surrounded by thick smoke on the bleak Cornwall landscape, unable to see even a

90

few feet ahead of him, overwhelmed by fear, is loaded with the complex significance of the awareness of 'imminent extinction.' The encounter with the pensioner in the tea-shop guarded by two formidable females adds existential evidence to symbolic apprehension.

The relationship between Biswas and the narrator outlines two distinct worlds, "One dead, the other powerless to be born." In the meantime individuals aware of this situation seek to stretch the limits of their society as a response to a sense of danger:

> But tranquillity recedes. The barracoon is over-crowded; the escape routes are closed. The people are disaffected and have no sense of danger.[*]

Mr. Biswas, for no fault of his own, is born an outsider. The pandit who comes to name him,

> In Tara's house he was respected as a Brahmin and pampered; yet as soon as the ceremony was over and he had taken his gift of money and cloth and left, he became once more only a labourer's child—*father's occupation: labourer* was the entry in the birth certificate F.Z. Ghany had sent—living with a penniless mother in one room of a mud hut. And throughout life his position was like that. As one of the Tulsi sons-in-law and as a journalist he found himself among people with money and sometimes with graces; with them his manner was unforcedly easy and he could summon up luxurious instincts; but always, at the end, he returned to his crowded, shabby room. (49)

Responsibility for the welfare of others, first his mother and later his wife and children, is forced upon him. Body and soul are in conflict for in his society there are not enough choices which can satisfy both at the same time. Sign-painting channelizes his artistic inclinations but is only a casual occupation. Happy in it, it ironically leads him to Hanuman House and marriage with Shama--accidental, manipulated and enslaving:

> The world was too small, the Tulsi family too large. He felt trapped.
> How often, in the years to come, at Hanuman House or in the house at Shorthills or in the house in Port of Spain, living in one room, with some of his children sleeping on the next bed, and Shama, the prankster, the server of black cotton stockings, sleeping downstairs with the other children, how often did Mr. Biswas regret his weakness, his inarticulateness, that evening! How often did he try to make events appear grander, more planned and less absurd than they were! (91)

In trying to set up an independent home with Shama we see Biswas's greatest struggles against threatened poverty and economic dependence on the Tulsis. Mrs. Tulsi's arrogant domination over those whom she shelters is too much for this independent, sensitive and relatively more educated son-in-law who cherishes secret romantic dreams of heroism and adventure nurtured by his reading of the English classics. Fantasy though it is, it enables him to survive the Tulsi overlordship and pragmatism:

> The organization of the Tulsi house was simple. Mrs. Tulsi had only one servant, a Negro woman who was called Blackie by Seth and Mrs. Tulsi, and Miss Blackie by everyone else. Miss Blackie's duties were vague. The daughters and their children swept and washed and cooked and served in the store. The husbands, under Seth's supervision, worked on the Tulsi land, looked after the Tulsi animals, and served in the store. In return they were given food, shelter and a little money; their children were looked after; and they were treated with respect by people outside because they were connected with the Tulsi family. Their names were forgotten; they became Tulsis. There were daughters who had, in the Tulsi marriage lottery, drawn husbands with money and position;

these daughters followed the Hindu custom of living with
their husband's families, and formed no part of the Tulsi
organization. . . .

Mr. Biswas had no money or position. He was expected to
become a Tulsi. At once he rebelled.''(97)

As long as the Tulsis aid him to 'paddle his own canoe' each attempt
to set up his own, ends in failure. For his literary aspirations to read
and write are not an integral part of the independence they offer him
as a shopkeeper at the Chase and as a sub-overseer at the Greenvale
sugar estate. His sensibility revolts against bookkeeping and the
squalor in which the labourers live:

In all Mr. Biswas lived for six years at The Chase, years so
squashed by their own boredom and futility that at the end
they could be comprehended in one glance. But he had aged.
. . .

Though he never ceased to feel that some nobler purpose
awaited him, even in this limiting society, he gave up reading
Samuel Smiles. . . . But now, though his philosophical books
gave him solace, he could never lose the feeling that they were
irrelevant to his situation. The books had to be put down. The
shop awaited; money problems awaited; the road outside was
short, and went through flat fields of dull green to small, hot
settlements.

And at least once a week he thought of leaving the shop,
leaving Shama, leaving the children, and taking that road.
(182-83)

In this account of the growth of Biswas from childhood to
adulthood we see the emerging pattern of his personality in conflict
with his society: his determination to be himself, shamed, yet not
submitting to the ridicule and humiliations thrust on him even by
Shama and his children as they view him with Tulsi eyes. Gradually
becoming estranged he moves inwards, becoming aware of objective reality as an increasingly threatening environment:

> He was rocking hard on the creaking board one night when ne
> thought of the power of the rockers to grind and crush and
> inflict pain, on his hands and toes and the tenderer parts of his
> body. He rose at once in agony, covering his groin with his
> hands, sucking hard on his teeth, listening to the chair as,
> rocking, it moved sideways along the cambered plank. The
> chair fell silent. He looked away from it. On the wall he saw
> a nail that could puncture his eye. The window could trap and
> mangle. So could the door. (229)

He cannot evaluate it rationally so that during his final nervous
breakdown in his collapsing half-built Greenvale house during the
thunderstorm even the ants, the moths and the dribbling tar assume
threatening surrealistic shapes. Only Anand's chanting is the last
link with reality. This contact is also broken when Anand, also
frightened, cannot carry on. He is carried to Hanuman House and
there, with great care, he recovers. With his physical recovery,
without the pressure of financial need, he feels free to meditate. He
acquires a certain distance from himself and appreciates fully, for
the first time, the comfort and security of Hanuman House-- 'Je
vens d'lue' as Ralph Singh says. (250) This is the moment from
which we measure Biswas's recovery and entry into his larger
society. Earning a living is not now only a necessity and an
unpleasant duty, but an aspect of his personality and acquires the
contours of an adventure. It is a move towards wholeness, of
coincidence of vision and action:

> He was going out into the world, to test it for its power to
> frighten. The past was counterfeit, a series of cheating acci-
> dents. Real life, and its especial sweetness, awaited; he was
> still beginning. (305)

Deserting his family at the Tulsis, convinced that as always
they would be well-looked after, he journeys to Port of Spain. There
he stays with Dehuti till he is able to locate a suitable job. He comes

to journalism via his talents as a sign-painter; now his artistic inclination becomes an actual condition of his freedom, economic and personal. He becomes a reporter on the *Sentinel*. Mr. Burnett, his boss, senses his talents and employs him accordingly in writing sensational news. He finds ample scope for his sense of adventure and romance in his literary writing and the physical mobility his profession requires--ultimately combining both in his role of Scarlet Pimpernel. He gains notoriety on the island as well as a substantial pay packet. Thus established he brings his family to Port of Spain and educates his children, especially Anand, in the best schools. The snag is that they occupy a Tulsi house, though they pay rent. Even here the authority, solidity and power of Tulsi money induces in him, periodically, the greatest insecurity, for it is a constant reminder of his own relative security extracted from an unwilling society where jobs are scarce and competition is great. Mr. Burnett's sack revives his fears and everyday he expects to be "summoned to mysterious rooms and told by their secure occupants that his services were no longer required." (368) The policies of the new management, curbing the style of its reporters, again reduce Biswas to a mechanical existence:

> Now, writing words he did not feel, he was cramped, and the time came when he was not sure what he did feel. He had to note down ideas and juggle them into place. He wrote and rewrote, working extremely slowly, nagged by continual headaches, completing his articles only to meet the Thursday deadline. The results were laboured, dead, incapable of giving pleasure except to the people written about. (375)

In the meantime they move once more to a joint family existence at Shorthills. It is shortlived and disastrous. Biswas once more constructs a house for himself on Tulsi land with Tulsi timber a short distance from the main house but hidden from it by trees. The house creates more problems for the family than it solves. And when Biswas, in an effort to clear the bush around it, burns it down, Shama and the children are quite relieved. Once more they move to

95

Port of Spain and occupy two rooms in the Tulsi house, the others being taken over by other sons-in-law. Mrs. Tulsi finally joins the establishment. Unhappy and humiliated, Biswas ignores her hints about vacating the overcrowded house, for he has nowhere to go. Housing is short and rents are high, food scarce and expensive. He does not have enough money to buy himself a house and Shama is as antagonistic as ever. '"'Yes,' Shama would say. 'I suppose if it wasn't for my family you would have a grass roof over your head.'"' (377) Insults and humiliations pile up; the children also want to leave and finally Mrs. Tulsi orders Biswas out of the house telling him 'to go to hell.'

He buys a handsome-looking house on loan and moves into it. Settling in becomes a great adventure for the family. As the children and Shama discover its shortcomings and defects Biswas realizes that once again he has been duped: he has made a bad bargain. Though defective and mortgaged it eventually gives the greatest satisfaction to the Biswas family. For the first time in their lives they find themselves together under the same roof, in accord with one another, and far enough from Tulsi taunts to forget them. They discover their relationships with each other as members of one family instead of leading a life of divided loyalties; it becomes the recipient of and reflects their existence:

> Soon it seemed to the children that they had never lived anywhere but in the tall square house in Sikkim Street. From now their lives would be ordered, their memories coherent. The mind, while it is sound, is merciful. And rapidly the memories of Hanuman House, The Chase, Green Vale, Shorthills, the Tulsi house in Port of Spain would become jumbled, blurred; events would be telescoped, many forgotten. (581)

Shama, who has gradually begun to share the economic burden of the house by her various schemes to earn money, now tries to help Biswas 'to paddle his own canoe,' and learns to depend on him instead of running off to her mother as she always did earlier. The children branch off into fruitful careers from this house. Biswas buys a car. Anand and Savi go to England for further studies. This house also becomes the scene of unhappiness when Biswas has a stroke and has to be hospitalized. It becomes the expression of their love as Kamla, Myna and Shama prepare it to welcome Biswas back from the hospital, recovered and able to go back to work. Secure on his own piece of earth and in the possession of his family, his neurotic fears regarding his own incapacity and entrapment by the Tulsis disappear. His powers of imagination and observation now become the source of a full and whole life. His personality subsumes the house, the garden, the car and the furniture. But his pleasure in them is intensified by a sense of sharing them with his family. Each item has a personality which expresses itself in its history, recalled with pleasure. They are no longer mere possessions over which he gloats in miserly loneliness erecting them as barriers against his existential insecurity. This is the house in which he dies in peace and triumph. For he has provided adequate shelter for Shama and the children.

His faith in himself is justified as he witnesses the gradual deterioration, literal and literary, of Tulsi power. The Tulsi family disintegrates and reorganizes itself into smaller, independent units. The narrator describes these changes as simultaneous with Mrs. Tulsi's deteriorating condition and approaching death. Shekhar, the elder Tulsi son, quarrels with Seth, who now feels that he is being treated as an outsider. He moves with his family into a house in the next street to Hanuman House and purchases a store which is bigger and better than theirs and threatens to buy up the whole family as well. Loyalties being openly divided, some other sons-in-law move out as well. This fracture is compounded by Shekhar's move to his in-laws's family after his marriage to Dorothy, a Christian of a rich Port of Spain family. Later they set up a separate home, something unthought of when the novel begins. W.C. Tuttle buys his own home and after Owad's return from England Biswas is forced to move away from the Tulsi clan into his own home. New ideas adulterate the old and pressures relax.

In itself Biswas's victory is insignificant but measured

against what has happened to the Tulsis, it assumes importance as a precursor of a new order. For his triumph, Biswas pays with his life--for he dies young, prematurely aged, sick, exhausted, receiving little or no recognition but much humiliation from his society for his sincere efforts to organize it closer to the heart's desire. A second stroke and a longer stay in hospital leaves him unfit for work and he is sacked by the *Sentinel*, which however continues to send a free copy of the paper till the time of his death. With no cause left to fight, a mounting debt on his house, without an income, he is once more, as he began, alone and unimportant. Life becomes absurd as he lives in a vacuum. All that is meaningful, the presence of Anand and Savi, is once more out of reach:

> But the debt remained. Four thousand dollars. Like a buffer at the end of a track, frustrating energy and ambition. Beyond the *Sentinel* there was nothing. . . . Living had always been a preparation, a waiting. And so the years had passed; and now there was nothing to wait for.
> Except the children. . . .
> He missed Anand and worried about him. Anand's letters, at first rare, became more and more frequent. . . . Anand's letters grew rare again. There was nothing Mr. Biswas could do but wait. Wait for Anand. Wait for Savi. Wait for the five years to come to an end. Wait. Wait. (586-87)

Waiting becomes a form of hope which keeps despair and neurosis at bay.

Biswas's contrary emotional states during his last months of life are the consequence not only of his strokes but of a lifetime of struggle and unrelieved tension made bearable by his indomitable spirit, his irascible sense of humour and a few gratifying successes. For Biswas release is just a state of being at peace with his surroundings, of not having to struggle anymore. Waiting, though a tragic, reducing experience, acquires a note of peace at the centre of his pathos. Released from the Tulsis, the narrator shows him trapped in his own home by his material inadequacies and his emotional dependence on his children. A further release for him is once more an imaginative and philosophical situation. A coherent vision disarms and places in perspective his material inadequacies so that they no longer assume the shape and threat of the black snakes chasing after him in his dreams. We see release from absurdity for this man whose energies have been fully deployed in wresting from life material respectability and an identity in consonance with his sense of dignity in death. Struggling to give meaning to his material existence, any thoughts about life beyond death would be as absurd as the talk of old men who gather in the front of Hanuman House in the early afternoons to talk about returning to India. They know they never will but it makes their present life more acceptable. The ultimate trap is the vast gap between struggle, ambition and actual achievement; the energy spent in the struggle to survive, to avoid failure, is out of all proportion to a man's actual achievement. It is the tenacity of the struggle that gives the 'little man' heroic proportions and releases him and us from the pettiness of our lives.

The prologue and the epilogue place "in parentheses" the chronological narrative of Biswas's life. As evidence of the critical synthesizing consciousness of the narrator they not only summarize the actual dramatic journey of Biswas from society to social reality but also clearly indicate his ironic, rational, existential bias. In the narrative Biswas and the narrator journey side by side. But the prologue and the epilogue belong to the narrator alone. They represent the third person narrator's effort at autobiographical simulation of Biswas's life without the use of first person narration as in *The Mimic Men*.

The chronological narrative stresses the arduousness and the interminable length of the journey. South Trinidad assumes continental proportions, its account covering nearly six hundred pages. The prologue focuses on the enlargement of consciousness as a consequence of maturity and experience. Here the rational consciousness of the narrator whittles down the distance a man need travel between society and social reality if thought and meditation and not passion and sensitivity alone form an integral part of his personality. The links between the Tulsi house, the house in Sikkim Street and 'one's portion of earth' are established in one sentence which forms a complete paragraph:

> But bigger than them all was the house, his house.
> How terrible it would have been, at this time, to be without it: to have died among the Tulsis, amid the squalor of that large, disintegrating and indifferent family; to have left Shama and the children among them, in one room; worse, to have lived without even attempting to lay claim to one's portion of the earth; to have lived and died as one had been born, unnecessary and unaccommodated. (13-14)

A perspective is established for the reader which no degree of sympathy for Biswas can dislodge. Unsupported by a vision of the larger world, his efforts to leave a mark on it naturally enough end in absurdity. The epilogue expands upon the most significant experience of Biswas's life: the experience of absurdity, of non-feeling and non-meaning and waiting, which cancels out an hitherto intensely passionate and aggressive existence. It also focuses for the reader the significance of this experience as the starting point of the narrative. Biswas's death, interpreted existentially, makes him an authentic member of the human community and an account of his life has universal implications.

The novel viewed as an interplay of the growing social and existential awareness of the narrator and protagonist dramatizes the strangling hold of a modern society on its individual members. Biswas's Hindu society, "driftwood" on Trinidad's colonial shores, is doubly insecure and anchorless. Shifting between Hindu ritual and an imported brand of Western philosophy and life-styles its form survives only through authoritarian control which demands conformity and obedience. Continuity is its underlying urge and any desire by its individual members to create within it an area of privacy and personal dignity is seen as a desire to alter it. Their yet amorphous creative and constructive urges are promptly crushed. Biswas succeeds insofar as he is able to widen his subjective and

100

familial horizons. The narrator succeeds in presenting his dilemma as a contemporary phenomenon. A personal family life and self-awareness as the knowledge of one's limitations are the basic design of the social reality which forms a desirable backdrop to this drama, unrealized but there. It is the difference between the death notice devised for himself: "ROVING REPORTER PASSES ON" and the actual one which announced his death in the *Sentinel*: "JOURNALIST DIES SUDDENLY." (589) It is his unfinished story:

"ESCAPE"
by M. Biswas

'At the age of thirty-three, when he was already the father of four children. . . .' Sometimes his hero had a Western name; he was then faceless, but tall and t road-shouldered; he was a reporter and moved in a world derived from the novels Mr. Biswas had read and films he had seen. None of these stories was finished, and their theme was always the same. The hero, trapped into marriage, burdened with a family, his youth gone, meets a young girl. She is slim, almost thin, and dressed in white. She is fresh, tender, unkissed; and she is unable to bear children. Beyond the meeting the stories never went. (344-45)

In *Mr. Stone and the Knights Companion*[7] the narrator describes the humanizing of Mr. Stone within a society which had dehumanized him. He builds up an expanding reality by subjectively rounding out an essentially flat and static character. Mr. Stone arrives at a sense of wholeness through a probing, questioning and observing attitude, which releases him from the congealed state into which 'habit' had forced him.

Mr. Stone, a bachelor of sixty-two years, just three years from retirement from his job in the firm of Excal, lives alone in his own house in a respectable suburb of London. With a bachelor fastidiousness, everything and every act has its proper place and time in

101

his life. Routine, system and neutrality are the watchwords of his life. His daily routine identifies time and place as the polarities between his office and his cosily shabby home whose solitude he cherishes after a noisy day outside. His outward and inward journey are extensions of his home and office. His knowledge of his streets is limited to his awareness of the cats that roam around in it. The only journey home to be described in some detail by the narrator in Stone's walk home on the particular Thursday afternoon when there is a transport strike.

The neighbourhood remains unfamiliar to him. He keeps it at a safe distance by divesting it of all individuality. Those neighbours whose activities he cannot help viewing through the bathroom window are labelled as the Male and the Monster for they happily indulge their human impulses and seem positively indecent to Stone. The tree in the school yard, less disturbing, receives his indulgent attention. Its seasonal changes and yearly growth awaken no response in him except as ''a reminder of the even flowing of time, of his mounting experience, his lengthening past.'' (17)

The days of the week are distinguished by the dresses Miss Menzies wears to work. She has a particular dress for each day and the routine never varies. His annual rituals, vigorously practised, of summer holidays in Europe, Christmas vacations with his sister, Olive, and Christmas parties at the Tomlinsons and his weekly ritual of a free Thursday, it being Mrs. Millington's day off, have so effectively disarmed time that its existential potential has been defused. Having created his magic dome he lives in a timeless, placeless eternity sealed in by habit. Intrusions and variations are not tolerated. No one visits him. All perspective has been abolished and a literal world established:

> Cherishing the past in this way, he cherished his appearance. He was a big man, well-made; his clothes sat well on him. The performance of a habitual action he never rushed, whether it was the putting on of a coat or the unfolding of a paper after dinner. . . . And he cultivated his habits. He shaved the right side of his face first; he put on his right shoe first. . . . He

bought two evening newspapers, the *News* and the *Standard*, from a particular vendor at Victoria; without glancing at them he folded them and put them in his briefcase; they were not to be read on the train . . . but were to be read at leisure after dinner, the news to be savoured not as news, for he instantly forgot most of what he read, but as part of a *newspaper*, something which day by day produced itself for his benefit during this after-dinner period, an insulation against the world out of which it arose. (16)

He possesses a material and emotional security and freedom from obligations which Biswas would envy. Like Biswas he is possessed of a certain restless energy, but unlike him he has no effective society on which to exercise it. For though, like Biswas, he has been an outsider to his society, unlike him, his present relationship to it is a consequence of his rejection of it. He has never felt the need for it. He is healthy and active and has taken to gardening for the exercise it affords him. His mind is busy either with figures and calculations or with fantasies which take concrete shape on Thursdays when he carves houses out of fresh loaves of bread or straightens out silver paper from cigarette cartons collecting unmanageable piles or chops up cheese into cubes to destroy cats. Even his freedom is carefully pigeonholed! His favourite fantasies, through repetition, have also taken on the colouring of an habitual performance:

It was in the empty house, on these occasions of Miss Millington's absence, that he found himself prey to fancies which he knew to be grotesque but which he ceaselessly indulged. He thought of moving pavements: he saw himself, overcoated and with his briefcase, standing on his private moving strip and gliding along, while walkers on either side looked in amazement. He thought of canopied streets for winter, the pavements perhaps heated by that Roman system he had seen at Bath. He was able to fly. (8)

103

Mrs. Millington, his housekeeper, is valued like the house, for remaining discreet and unobtrusive.

The novel opens on an uneasy note with Mr. Stone, on his return from office, discovering an intruder in his house when he expected complete solitude, it being Thursday. He reacts almost superstitiously as if the cat, on his darkened staircase, challenges his ownership of the house. The cat disappears as rapidly as a hallucination caused by the change from the light of the outside world to the darkened interior. Calm returns. He takes immediate steps for the destruction of the cat should it return. The chopping up of cheese to decoy the cat into the toilet would arouse our amusement at this neurotic bachelor's tantrums were it not followed by the scene of a sinister Mr. Stone sitting on the lavatory bowl with a poker to crush out its brains, seeing visions besides of scalding it with boiling oil or water. Unusually, his latent aggressiveness and fear of society surface and from now onwards a series of events are described which turn turtle Mr. Stone's long and well-supervised past:

> But this morning the familiarity of the scene did not soothe him. He felt only a faint unease, whose origin he couldn't place and which, persisting, gave him a twinge of alarm, for it seemed that all the ordered world was threatened. (18)

He can find no categorical explanation for the uneasiness and sense of fear which accompany the performance of routine activity. For having left his struggles behind him, literally and metaphorically, he considers himself as one who has very deftly carved out his 'portion of the earth' to suit his needs. Now he intuits that the walls of his citadel are shaky.

The narrative is structured within a dual framework: the historical and existential. The narrator briefly recounts Stone's early emotional disaster to provide a framework for the unbelievable isolation he has imposed on himself and his orientation to the past. It has become a self-perpetuating automatic process so that his life has become mechanical. His sensitive, imaginative, adolescent nature had responded traumatically to the experience of loss,

104

insecurity and pain at his mother's death. He turned to his sister and after a brief and happy companionship she let him down by getting married and having a baby girl. The brother-sister relationship is restored somewhat after Olive loses her husband. But the presence of the growing child, Gwen, petulant and spoilt, is a continuing threat to Mr. Stone's peace of mind. He has been repeatedly betrayed by the women in his life and his response has been withdrawal from life itself.

This firm psychological-historical set of mind is challenged by the presence of the cat, the intruder in the darkened hall on a Thursday afternoon on his return from office, so that the existential framework of the narrative as the conflict between self and society, in which the latter dominates, is activated by the historical. The narrator encompasses a period of three eventful years in Stone's life within a psychological moment of change which represents a great personal upheaval and the growth of a personal vision. This subjective change is framed within two accounts of his encounter, in almost similar circumstances, with the neighbour's cat. The day of the week is the same, the hall and the staircase are the same. The cat is there and the house is empty. But there is a difference which makes all the difference in his life. Then he was presumably returning to an empty house. Now, though Mrs. Millington is retired, he expects Margaret to be home, and the act, the offspring of the earlier one, has already been categorized as 'his.' The narrator thus reduces the significance of subjective life by juxtaposing it with the too solid, external, literal world, unaware, indifferent if not patronizing and hostile. In Margaret's words Stone's insight, so painfully gained, is "a lota rubbish." (116) And she, the person closest to Stone, undoubtedly represents his effective social environment in the novel.

The narrator builds up the mood of growing irritability and despair by letting us see Mr. Stone trying to focus and so categorize his present uneasiness. In the process he reassesses the people and situations he had so far taken for granted; they gradually become part of his existential landscape: the carefully isolated past is moving into the present and integrating with it.

105

All his musings eventually lead to thoughts of death, loss and disintegration. It strikes him that the poster in the London underground train advertising Spring tourism uses language which emphasizes the cold and dark of a seemingly endless city winter. His effort at light off-colour jokes at the Tomlinsons's Christmas party is met with a reproving silence. He has not appreciated the fact that Mrs. Springer is recently widowed. Mrs. Millington is old and "must one day die"; but now her old age takes on a personal meaning: she was "soon to die." (19) The vision of the deformed boy in the dimly-lit library entrance, almost repeating his initial experience with the cat in the hallway in his house, frightens him so that he went "scuttling home to Miss Millington in what was almost fear." (21) And this year even his visit to Olive does not dissipate his uneasiness. It only succeeds in suppressing it for the time being.

In this state any distraction is welcome which carries the pretence of his former carefree life. He therefore welcomes Mrs. Springer's invitation to tea. Her regard restores his confidence. And though he thinks that Earls Court is "a disreputable, overcrowded area," (26) he goes. In return he invites Mrs. Springer home for tea. He is helping actively in breaking down his 'habit' barriers, as if there are two Mr. Stones, one conspiring against the other. And so the outside world, like the cat, intrudes into his privacy. Before he can do much about it he finds himself married to Margaret Springer. (One is reminded of Biswas's predicament at Hanuman House, similarly cornered by Mrs. Tulsi and Seth). Marriage, however, leads to new fears and anxieties which mingle with and intensify the old uneasiness. His marital status leads to a distinct change in the established cordialities at the office. The young girls no longer pet him or flirt with him. The irreverent jokes of his colleagues only remind him of his age and his approaching retirement. A community has dissolved. Even the tree in the yard turns hostile, reminding him of the end.

But beneath the apparent calm which marriage had once more brought to him, there grew a new appreciation of time. It was

106

flying by. It was eating up his life. . . . Every ordered week reminded him of failure, of the uncreative years once so comfortingly stacked away in his mind. Every officeless Sunday sharpened his anxiety, making him long for Monday and the transient balm of the weekdays, false though he knew their fullness to be, in spite of the office diary he had begun to keep, tabulating appointments, things to be done, to flatter himself that he was busily and importantly occupied.

The tree, changing, developing with the year, made its point every day. (45-46)

The narrator stresses the different sensibilities of Margaret and Stone as they settle down to a married life: she literal and demanding, playing 'house' with gusto, forcing on him her pre-formed notions of the man of the world, the master, the husband, and the business executive; he gentle, pliable yet resentful of her harmless insincerities and unable to identify his roles with his personality, feeling cramped and unhappy. The frictions and tensions mount and keep bubbling beneath the calm routine of the house. His reaction is to escape from home, from office, from nothingness. But, as for Biswas and Ferdinand, there is nowhere to go:

Now there was no escape.

From his role as their brave bull, going forth day after day to 'business' (Miss Menzies's word, which was Margaret's as well), he hoped to find rest in the office. But rest there was none, for increasingly his manner, to his disquiet, reflected his role. (34)

Then the decision to take a holiday-cum-honeymoon trip offers temporary release.

Their trip to Cornwall, instead of the customary one to Europe, a 'delicate' reminder of the need to economise because retirement is only eighteen months away, reveals to each the extent of their mutual dependence. In this unfamiliar rural environment,

107

where nature dominates, used as he is to man-dominated city life, Stone once more senses his own frailty. His fashionable city clothes make him feel conspicuous and vulnerable. He cannot avoid seeing reminder of death and decay:

> Once on a bare cliff they came upon a dead fox, as whole as the living animal, no marks of death or violence on it, lying on its side as if in sleep, its fur blown about by the wind. (48)

He panics when his silent guide gestures to them to follow him into the smoke of the fire in the field which they must cross on their way to St. Ives. Imagination, unfettered by routine presences, dislocates reason. The fire, like the cat and the deformed boy, is an insubstantial, hallucinatory experience:

> Behind the wall they stood, watching the fire. It came right up to the wall and before their eyes burnt itself out. The smoke was dissipated in the air. And it was as if there had been no fire, and all that had happened a hallucination. . . .
>
> Mr. Stone never doubted that the incident could be rationally and simply explained. But that hallucinatory moment, when earth and life and senses had been suspended, remained with him. It was like an experience of nothingness, an experience of death. (50)

A more solid reminder of his ultimate condition is his subsequent meeting with the mousey, recently retired man and his women companions at Miss Chichester's teashop where they are joined by the Dutch mountaineer and his girlfriend. Strangers all, they try to conjure up a matey, holiday mood. The whole scene, out of a Pinter play, is incongruous, almost absurd; their conversation only augments dread, and loneliness. The tie that binds them is the retirement gift watch which is passed around from hand to hand. Stone's need of Margaret contains the germ of imprisonment.

From his great despair germinates the determination to survive. His existential experience matures into a creative idea which later in "licked into shape" by Whymper into the scheme of the Knights Companion. It meets with the boss's approval and Mr. Stone experiences the triumph of success. He moves into a new office, with brand-new furniture, in a new building. He gets a salary raise and his promotion is mentioned in the house magazine; and "there was also a photograph." (64) Margaret renovates the house and gives parties. That Christmas they are the chief guests at the Tomlinsons's annual party.

However, the modern world, in the shape of Whymper, as an assistant, intrudes into his life. The latter's values triumph over those of Stone who is made to realize how outdated he is. Whymper begins by being his friend; he sees the commercial possibilities of the scheme he facetiously refers to as the society "for the protection of the impotent male." (66) He develops it as an advertising stunt for the firm, 'riding to success' on Stone's back. Stone sees himself displaced by Whymper, young and modern, at the office and also at home where Margaret welcomes his attentions. And once again disillusioning reality forces its way through the aura of a created world. The case of the Prisoner of Muswell Hill, an Excal pensioner, imprisoned to the point of insanity by his daughter, connects with the meeting with the pensioner in the tea shop guarded and reduced by his female companions. He sees reflected in these situations his own possible condition. He further notices that Grace is looking younger after Tomlinson's death and is enjoying life. The two strands of existential despair, women and insecurity, continue to link and reinforce each other.

In spite of himself he becomes more and more isolated, not realizing the extent to which he is protected and supported by Margaret, and internally, by a growing appreciation of his surroundings, which yield a literary and philosophical understanding of life. "Even as Mr. Stone watched, the cat woke, stretched itself in a slow, luxurious, assured action, and rose. It was as if the world was awakening from winter." (105) His mind is flexing, growing and changing: his emerging vision of a continuing order now gives security and confidence to counteract his physical ageing. And so his neighbourhood closes in on him becoming a part of his reality.

He even learns the names of his long-ignored and detested neighbours from Margaret. The Midgeley's cat becomes his own black cat. His feelings are once more engaged and pain can be borne. 'His' black cat is destroyed. Its mate's frenzy in the street communicates the news to him. But he also sees its offspring in the same old place outside the bathroom window. And now he is not afraid to feel and think, even though feeling exposed arouses ridicule and ideas put into action, manipulated to serve selfish ends, become impure. He learns to accommodate the act of betrayal as a human not merely a personal fact.

Meanwhile in the office Whymper continues to make life difficult for him and he feels more and more excluded and unnecessary:

> In the routine of the office, as in the rhythm of the seasons, he could no longer participate. It all went without reference to himself. Soon it would go on without his presence . . . his earlier petulance had given way to weariness and indifference and then at last to a distaste for the office which was like fear. (119)

So that retirement almost seems a pleasant proposition--an escape. Like bad luck, Whymper tags him even in his personal life when he seduces his willing niece, Gwen, and they elope. Disgusted, Stone sees the Male-Monster syndrome become a reality in his life. His ultimate professional betrayal, which brings his personal crisis to a head, is when the office boy, on this particular Thursday afternoon, brings to his notice the announcement in the *World's Press News*, of Whymper's appointment as publicity director at Gow's. One of his achievements mentioned is his success as PRO at Excal. He is stated as the architect of the successful Knights Companion Scheme for its retired pensioners. His identity thus snatched away Stone feels totally annulled. He leaves the office only to find that there is a transport strike in London. And so Stone learns to walk for the first time, instead of flying over the city or travelling along swiftly moving staircases. He appreciates the sense of well-being and exhaustion the physical exertion causes. Just the act of walking and looking around, of being aware of the physical life of the city--its variety, its gaiety, its corruptibility--and having the time to meditate and reflect dulls his pain. He realizes the astonishing power as well as the frailty of his own body: its capacity to feel pain and its power to numb and tolerate it as well. Confidence restored, released by thought from the one-dimensional world of habit, which had hedged in his fear of pain and rejection, he is free to love. He has come a long way from waiting in fear and hatred for the cat to waiting in patience and acceptance for Margaret. As for Biswas, waiting becomes a condition and a period of hope in what seems to be a hopeless situation.

The novel is as highly and as rhythmically structured as a poem. As the narrative progresses it gains in symbolic complexity till Mr. Stone becomes a particular kind of everyman at a certain decisive stage in his life. Survival means battling with his problems and he emerges victorious. The narrator stresses Stone's subjective/objective alienation intensified by the society in which he lives. He focuses on the dissociation between body and mind in Mr. Stone's consciousness. Analytical, thoughtful, sensitive and imaginative he uses his faculties not to live creatively and fully but to dull an unbearable pain and to an induced self paralysis which leads to a bodyless existence. The novel expands upon the extremely slow and painful process of recovery and rediscovery of the world; this relinking of the body and mind occurs as a consequence of a need--fear of nonexistence and the desire for recognition. The threat to the body rediscovers it for him.

No idea introduced into the novel is wasted by the narrator. The framework of argument and symbolism is spare, clear and relevant. Any reference to Spring can arouse the winter-bound, hibernating Englishman out of his lethargy. "Those who doubt the coming of Spring:" (20)--a typical contemporary technique of salesmanship, selling nature to a civilization that can appreciate only what can be paid for. (Nature is a commodity, a material pleasure not an existential understanding of life.) It becomes for Stone an intuitive apprehension when, as towards the end he says, shyly, "I mean, don't you think it's just the same with us? That we too will have our spring?" (116) A man has once more realized sympathy with the ground he walks on. Paradox and irony extend the symbolic tension of the novel to its limits. Mr. Stone has lived a bleak and cold youth and manhood, in a damp, dark and lonely house in the company of a woman devoid of all female charm. Impotence characterizes his existence. And then, later, close to the winter of his life, unbelievably, a brief spring rejuvenates him.

The novel's dialectics of existence/nonexistence, subjective/ objective, past/present, movement/stasis, defined by the new/old, old/young and dark/light syndrome, cover a wide range of existential facts in Stone's life: freedom/entrapment, security/freedom/ adventure, insecurity/home/stasis, life/death/death-in-life/life-in-death, man/woman, man/nature, male/female, male/man/gentleman, manhood/impotence, love/hatred. All these interlock and converge, towards the end, in Stone's double vision of man--of himself as the creator and the destroyer of his social universe. It is significant that Ralph Singh, the most aware third world personality in Naipaul's fiction, attributes this power to create or destroy not to man but to the sophisticated, cosmopolitan culture of London.[*] In man all polarities of thought, feeling, action and ideal become continuous and ambiguous along a moving spectrum of consciousness.

Stone's isolation from his milieu is an usual feature of contemporary cosmopolitan, industrial life. This, super-imposed on a natural human alienation which is at the same time a cultural and a personal bias, privacy being highly valued by the English, makes a direct unfiltered response to raw experience impossible. The narrator's exposition of Stone's situation enables Naipaul to give fictional shape to his concern with those conditions in contemporary society which hinder a man from attaining a 'fix on reality.'

Though a story about an elderly man's efforts to survive in a highly structured social set-up, society in this novel is materially absent when compared to the full-bodied garrulous world of Mr. Biswas. The narrator, as the objective artist who describes but does not question the reality he creates, becomes an aspect of Mr. Stone's

112

missing society. Its power to neutralize its potentially creative and useful members is all the more strongly realized in Mr. Stone's despairing sense of alienation whose roots are established in a psychological past. Like Biswas, Stone is never fully alive to the present except in the end through the narrator's sympathetic assessment and symbolic resolution of the narrative. Gripped by the past he lives in anticipating a possible future which, as a constant effort to evade involvement and pain, is shaped imaginatively like the past. Naipaul delineates a static society which either destroys or forces its members to live outside it. It thus defeats its own purpose besides making ineffective the rich social tradition which made it possible.

The symbolism in the novel enables Naipaul to present Stone as ultimately larger and stronger than his society, in his capacity to change by reflection on his present situation and imaginatively to link it with the larger universal social reality. His marriage is the replay of the age-old comic romance, indicative of mythic ritual, re-enacted in a contemporary setting in which psychological/subjective rather than physical/objective needs and traumas predominate.

These novels describe closed worlds. They reflect on the relationship between the homeless individual (only in a critical situation realizing the need for home), his society and the larger social reality. They develop the frightening paradox of a shrinking world progressively developing sophisticated techniques of 'functional' communication, and so trying to come closer to its material reality, by widening the gap between subjective and objective life, indirectly, creating the conditions which make 'human' communication increasingly difficult.⁺ Social reality, as an achieved personal vision, emphasizes the greater distance a man has to travel today between subjective and objective reality to arrive at a sense of wholeness. It is also with the greatest difficulty that a man, once alienated, can hope to reenter society.

In these novels one sees both society and individual alienated from the larger social reality whose presence, as stated earlier, is experienced as fantasy and the urge for a personal vision of life, because of a static relationship to the past. Biswas, mockingly, and

Stone, seriously, each caricatures his past society. The situations which highlight human need of the other--alienation, isolation and deprivation--are all present as concurrent causes in the personalities of Biswas and Stone. These conditions are inherent in a society which is highly structured and inflexible, inducing a similar personality structure in its members.

These novels mimic the concepts of home, family, femininity, masculinity, chivalry, charity and marriage. The whole contemporary cultural context is sustained by a role-playing of the past. A personal victory of a Stone or a Biswas has no significance for a society which is creatively non-existent. They do not succeed in leaving a mark on it. Their victories follow them to the grave. Survival defines itself as an awareness of continuity and the need for change. Existential despair, therefore, becomes a historical and societal phenomena and as such is a condition of hope.

Naipaul presents the personality with a literary potential entrapped in his societal reality which is presented as the most vicious single cause of alienation.[10] An irresponsible society, as a reductive agent, is a farce for its more sensitive, inquiring members. They can remain alive only when they cease to live in tune with themselves.[11] (It is a society in which material success and aesthetic development are opposed not integrated possibilities). For the assumptions underlying its self-perpetuation are the colonial attitudes of power and possession. It is a society which is unable to either provide sustenance for a creative existence or succour in times of crisis. Each society is a different configuration of social reality and both are seen to betray the possibilities of its individual members.

NOTES

1.   V.S. Naipaul, *India: A Wounded Civilization* (Harmondsworth: Penguin, 1979), p. 41.
2.   Cf. V.S. Naipaul, "London," *The Overcrowded Barracoon*

and other Articles (Harmondsworth: Penguin, 1976).

3.   Cf. Herbert Marcuse, *One Dimensional Man: Studies in the Ideology of Advanced Industrial Society* (London: Routledge and Kegan Paul, 1964), Preface, p. xvi.

4.   Cf. William Walsh, *V.S. Naipaul* (Edinburgh: Oliver and Boyd, 1973). See the next chapter for his discussion of the metaphor of the journey in *In a Free State.*

5.   V.S. Naipaul, *A House for Mr. Biswas* (Harmondsworth: Penguin, 1969), p. 590.

6.   *The Overcrowded Barracoon and Other Articles,* p. 309.

7.   V.S. Naipaul, *Mr. Stone and the Knights Companion* (Harmondsworth: Penguin, 1977).

8.   Cf. *The Mimic Men,* p. 52.

9.   Cf. *One Dimensional Man.* See the next chapter.

10. Cf. *Ibid.,* pp. 238-43.

11. *Ibid.,* p. 9. "The intellectual and emotional refusal 'to go along' appears neurotic and important."

Personal Reality and its Postulates:
Guerrillas; A Bend in the River

In the novels so far examined the awareness of the self in dialectical relationship to one's political and social reality is the underlying cause for the experience of entrapment and the consequent confrontations, conflicts and crises in the lives of Naipaul's protagonists. In *Guerrillas* and *A Bend in the River* the political and societal reality of the earlier novels is now incorporated within the powerful, all-embracing personal/existential reality of each of the characters. In their world, viewed through their eyes, politics and society and non-existent in the accepted sense, so that the internal and external, once antithetical, are now analogues. The external world of both novels is as chaotic, disordered, violent and almost deranged, as their mental landscapes are. This ferment, containing all the promise of creation, remains unresolved in these novels where it is dramatized as a destructive element. It is no longer possible for Salim to feel as Ralph Singh does:

> The city made by man but passed out of his control: break-down the negative reaction, activity the positive: opposite but equal aspects of an accommodation to a sense of place which, like memory, when grown acute, becomes a source of pain.[1]

Jane sinks in it. Roche and Salim survive through retreat.

In these two novels tension is maintained through implied paradox, the actual story becoming a narrative metaphor for a particular vision of the world. Each novel lays bare the emotional and passionate reality of despair and hysterical fear which underlies the contemporary human situation, ignored, dismissed or suppressed by the general euphoria and optimism generated by incalculable wealth and power. Naipaul reveals the vulnerability of a world which wastes its potential--the sense of a community gone wrong; the protagonist realizes himself as a victim of his environment:

Once it had been a respectable lower-class area. . . . But the community once contained in this area of greenery and red roofs and narrow lanes had exploded. Families still lived in certain houses; but many of the houses had become camping places, where young men looked for occasional shelter and an occasional meal, young men who at an early age had found themselves in the streets, without families, knowing only the older women of some houses as 'aunts.'

It was a community now without rules; and the area was now apparently without municipal regulation. Empty houselots had been turned into steel-band yards or open-air motor-repair shop; . . . The walls were scrawled, and sometimes carefully marked, with old election slogans, racial slogans, and made-up African names: . . . Humour, of a sort, was intended; and it seemed at variance with the words of threat and danger.[2]

You mustn't think it's bad just for you. It's bad for everybody. That's the terrible thing. It's bad for Prosper, bad for the man they gave your shop to, bad for everybody. Nobody's going anywhere. . . . Nothing has any meaning. That is why everyone is frantic. . . . The bush runs itself. But there is no place to go to. I've been on tour in the villages. It's a nightmare. All these airfields the man has built, the foreign companies have built--nowhere is safe.[3]

The terms in which these novels are structured, producing resonances which deepen the despair and gloom of the existential reality, vibrate obversely off-stage. The melodrama of petty heroics (historical as well as autobiographical), self-pity and physical violence (murders, torture, sadism) become an absurd tragedy as the narrator presents on the fringes of his protagonist's memories the awareness of an ordered past. Most of the real action of *Guerrillas* consists in characters talking nostalgically of the past and Salim's whole exercise consists in recalling a happier time when he was vital. The past they sought to escape from, to reject or alter is now a life-line in the destructive present, when the glamour of existenz has materialized into the paralysis of fear. The charm of distant places, of new and better worlds, dissipates as they realize that all places are the same place; they experience the same resistance to ideational living everywhere as well as discover the corrupt core of their own beings. (Having wasted time they become grabbers and opportunists of the moment. In Nazruddin's words: "You must always know when to pull out."' For moving in one direction only, literally and literarily, we see them exhausted, having soon reached the limits of their imaginative existence. The sense of being out of step with the times comes to Peter, Jane, Jim, Harry and other characters in *Guerrillas*. They all repeat at some point in their lives: 'It is too late.' The sense of time slipping is the impetus to action in *A Bend in the River:*

> They're going to kill everybody who can read and write, everybody who ever put on a jacket and tie,.... They're going to kill all the masters and all the servants.... They're going to kill and kill. They say it is the only way, to go back to the beginning before it's too late. (293)

We see lonely people searching for emotional richness ending up more alienated, insulated and ridden by fear if not hatred.

The narrator, able to manifest such paradoxical situations in novels in which meaning does not reside in the actual action, presents a clearer picture of himself as he seeks to hide behind his art, refining himself out of existence. The satiric/ironic self-aware narrator of earlier fiction trying to demonstrate that his third world protagonists are doomed to fail outside their narrow contexts because of their lack of self-awareness, now becomes part of his narrative context by refusing to assess it. In *Guerrillas* the narrator's sympathies are with all the characters. Whilst depicting their actions he simultaneously probes their psyches so that though they are critical of one another we see them as essentially victims of their situations: their greatnesses are measured against their failures. So that even the worst of them, the murderous gang leader, Jimmy, is a pathetic figure:

> She grew heavy; his strength became useless; and as he felt her fail a desolation began to grow on him. And then there was nothing except desolation. . . .
> Then he was lost, lost since the beginning of time. But time had no beginning and he was disembodied. He was nothing more than this sense of loss that grew deeper and deeper as he awakened to it. (243)

Salim in *A Bend in the River* is the well-defined protagonist of the novel. He weighs and assesses his various worlds. Yet Salim's voice, as that of the first person autobiographical narrator, is finally sympathetic and reductive. He is one of them. The adventurous son of a business and slave-owning family of considerable importance and antiquity on the east coast, he finally admits to Metty, his slave-servant, that he is scarcely able to take care of himself leave alone be responsible for him. His humiliations resolve themselves into a philosophical understanding of men:

> The world is what it is; men who are nothing, who allow themselves to become nothing, have no place in it. (9)

Naipaul shows that in a democratic world which stresses respect for the individual, survival is possible only in power groups. The individual not supported by power is always the hunted. The elements of choice and freedom, which gave dignity to existentialist thought, in today's political set-up, are no more the inherent right of the individualist but of the man in power. The Big Man in *A Bend in the River* plays fast and loose with men and machines, ideas and history. And Jimmy, the hakwai Chinese born in the back room of a Chinese Grocery, knows:

> They've got to support me, massa. Sablich's and everybody else. They've got to make me bigger. Because, if I fail--hmm. I'm the only man that stands between them and revolution, and they know it now, massa. That's why I'm the only man they're afraid of. . . . I'm the friend of every capitalist in the country. Everybody is my friend. (27)

In *Guerrillas* and *A Bend in the River*, Naipaul, through the omniscient, impersonal narrator, creates the personal, individualistic, self-aware, self-centred world of subjective reality. The characters, aware of an external world from which they are detached and free-floating, form a community of the fearful and the lost. They communicate with others only in so far as they understand the 'other' in terms of themselves, forming a single gigantic world personality. The distinction between the role of the protagonist and the other characters in the novel serves the artistic purpose of verisimilitude and authenticity. Thematically he merges into the quality of the life of the island and the town in the two novels respectively. The subjective realities of the nameless island and the unnamed town, as free-floating and dislocated as their inhabitants, are perceived to be as static, alienated and egotistical as the literal world of ritual and tradition or that confined by materialistic goals as embodied by the East coast life of Africa and the Ridge Community of the island respectively. Naipaul defines the motivation behind these realities as 'self-cherishing' or 'self-regard': the understanding of the self and the other in terms of power, possession and superiority rather than equality. The objective world of political and societal reality, as a thing in itself, does not exist in these novels. It is real and meaningful only in so far as it impinges on the experiential awareness of the character and forms the stuff of his subjective existence. Objective reality, mingled with the past and present, with aspiration and fantasy, is distorted and made

120

bizarre. If choice is the core of true existenz there does not seem much to choose between. At least the material world (money and automatic living) provides a foothold for survival for people who have exhausted their resources and know their limits. Transcontinental and international travel ends in repeated journeys between the ridge, the town and the Grange in *Guerrillas*. For Salim the decisive car rides are between his shop and flat and the residences of the various people with whom, out of his needs, he establishes ties, particularly with Yvette at the Domain. Heightened subjectivity, expanding the consciousness, has narrowed the scope of existenz. Freedom is in conflict with security and the novels end on a low note:

> Life in our town was arbitrary enough. Yvette seeing me as settled, with everything waiting for me somewhere, had seen her own life as fluid. She felt she wasn't prepared as the rest of us; she had to look out for herself. That was how we all felt, though: we saw our own lives as fluid, we saw the other man or person as solider. But in the town, where all was arbitrary and the law was what it was, *all* our lives were fluid. We none of us had certainties of any kind. Without always knowing what we were doing we were constantly adjusting to the arbitrariness by which we were surrounded. In the end we couldn't say where we stood.
>
> We stood for ourselves. We all had to survive. But because we felt our lives to be fluid we all felt isolated, and we no longer felt accountable to anyone or anything. That was what had happened to Mahesh. 'It isn't that there's no right and wrong here. There's no right! That was what had happened to me. It was the opposite of the life of our family and community on the coast. That life was full of rules. Too many rules; it was a pre-packed kind of life. Here I had stripped myself of all the rules. During the rebellion--such a long time ago--I had also discovered that I had stripped myself of the support the rules gave. To think of it like that was to feel myself floating and lost. And I preferred not to think about it--it was too much

like the panic you could at anytime make yourself feel if you thought hard enough about the *physical* position of the town in the continent, and your own place in that town. (206-7)

The implications of the novels emerge then from an examination of the relationship between the narrator and his art and the narrator and Naipaul. Each novel taken separately and the two taken together is a conjunction of contexts and perceptions of the existential and artistic consciousnesses of the narrator, Naipaul and the reader so that it creates a pictorial impact on the reader's mind, simultaneously becoming an interior monologue as he probes and questions his impressions.

The narrator's attitude to his art is moulded by his desire to create an effect of existential truth: how the subjective and objective, the contemporary individual and society interact to destroy rather than create. For him human reality is the only worthwhile evidence of the world we live in. He plants a flag for human reality in its potential not its actual achievement. He arouses sympathy by projecting on the reader's mind the dilemma of his protagonists who, in search of dignity, succeed only in realizing themselves as victims of their situation. Subjective living is a fight for survival as well as a retreat from the rapacious political and social world.

The narrators of both novels have lifted the material world to the symbolic to create a fable which is also a truth in which the reader can readily participate without bias. The narrator tells stories about insular and isolated societies and unimportant places to stress a general truth which requires this kind of treatment. They have evoked images of worlds externally hardly existent, their geography altered by a hysterical vision either of aridity as in *Guerrillas* or a choking fertility as in *A Bend in the River*, an inauthentic or absent history and a present which mocks social and political institutions: worlds suspended as Harry da Tunja's hammock between "the sea and the sky." (125) It is from such unnamed worlds that the disaffected penetrate, like guerrillas, into the solid world of power and importance. And it is in such places that the marginal men of the larger world seek a sense of belonging. Such

122

a situation can no longer be ignored or treated as marginal. The omniscient narrator of *Guerrillas* and the first person autobiographical narrator of *A Bend in the River* present the same vision objectively and subjectively: beneath the seeming contradictions, oppositions and conflicts between society and the individual there are not two realities but one.

The ironic vision of the novels that the reader achieves is a consequence of the "orchestration of perceptions."[5] Naipaul stands behind the narrator as the latter stands behind his characters in his dual role of involved witness and omniscient observer as they expose themselves and each other in 'last ditch stand' to force recognition of their materiality in their insubstantial worlds and so create a 'home' and 'a sense of belonging.' The narrator had 'refined himself out of existence' in order to involve the reader in the protagonist's situation. The reader feels directly the intensification of the mood as it grows and gathers force. Naipaul monitors this attempt by revealing the narrator's bias. The latter enhances the personality of his protagonist by subsuming the geographical and historical facts of the novel within his emotional atmosphere. The landscape becomes dependent on the 'mood' of the protagonist for its life and significance.

Naipaul reduces the protagonist by placing him and the events of his life in a wider context: he reintroduces historical, geographical and philosophical facts into the fiction. Kareisha and London are a constant reproach to Salim in his sub-lunar world in the town on the bend in the river. And his irreversible humiliation in the jail finally leads him back to the future he had run away from: that of an obedient husband and son managing a family business. Jimmy Ahmed's philosophical insight into the truth of third world reality reduces each self-involved character in the novel to a guerrilla fighting only for himself and that, as he says, is fighting for no cause at all. Jimmy reverts to the slave term 'massa' for the white man. Peter Roche returns, a defeated man, to anonymity and conformity, in London. Naipaul, in this manner, distancing the reader from the narrative forces him to question the reality the narrator would have him accept sympathetically. He does this to stress the complexity of contemporary life which does not yield to single-handed treatment or a simple vision.

In the racially and culturally complex societies of those two novels the narrator enables Naipaul to present a cross-section of a placeless world without intrinsic value in which the self is prostituted into a commodity to purchase 'a fix on reality.' Sex, violence, money, speech--the coins of exchange and communication--are all encompassed by the shopkeeper's jargon of buying and selling, the sense of misuse and waste and assessment of this world as a junkyard.

The characters achieve partial authenticity in their comprehension of themselves as dead ends; failures with possibility exhausted. This particular knowledge entraps them finally for it destroys the will to live. In these circumstances articulation and self-exposure as an act of self-assertion becomes a return journey through a partially known world: they restructure a remembered past to appear presentable to themselves and others. Survival and existence meet in the single-minded desire to 'save one's skin.'

The reader, exercising sympathy and judgement, is not coerced into a philosophical position. Instead, the overtly dialectical begins to lose its definite shape to become ambiguous and ironic. The narrator's vision merges into that of the protagonist and the reader views the novels through Naipaul's eyes. The disaffected existentialist protagonist, the victim of society, is also the destroyer of his community without which he cannot survive--for the victim seeks affirmation and asserts himself as the destroyer. This is the vision of Mr. Stone till, by an act of the will, he religiously converts it into a creative one. It is the question Ralph Singh raises: can the moment when the oppressor and oppressed change roles be pinpointed? Can these roles remain identifiable? Do they not merge or alter in the same person depending on the situation and context? This ambiguity of human motivation underlies Jim's roles in *Guerrillas* and orders the relationship between Ferdinand, Metty and Salim in *A Bend in the River*.

Though each novel portrays well-defined personalities who have separate existence--basically lonely people looking for human comfort--their vision is essentially social. The human dilemma evolves out of the conflict of cultures which themselves are not genuine as they have been prostituted by historical distortion or their inflexibility in the face of a growing and changing world. In these novels this confrontation of cultures takes place in recognizable third world countries which yet remain unreal to the people who congregate there. The 'whites' who have come to do 'good,' bring their burden of a secure superiority with them. The 'coloureds' reject their misrepresented cultures as inferior and backward. They also want to do 'good'-by climbing up the ladder and wishing to drag their countries up behind them. Such people starting out as rebels trap themselves in their roles. There are the usual drifters of each society who watch the way the wind blows, who live for themselves and who are considered free; they achieve a degree of success in their own terms. But in each case it is the 'land' which suffers, for ignored or exploited, it never acquires a personality of its own. The vision is that of Ralph Singh's which he expresses as a lack of sympathy between man and the earth he walks on. The naming of such a land, its cities, towns and streets becomes a futile exercise.

Though *Guerrillas* is an agonized parody of societal existence and *A Bend in the River* is a similar parody of individual existence because a man fails to measure accurately the distance between ideas and actuality, the novels together depict the close links between the individual and his social environment which itself is moulded by geography, history and man's greeds. The island and the town, the locales of the two novels respectively, have been important only as economic assets of the first world. The novels accentuate this unimportance: as the former, exhausted, and the latter, whose exploitation is becoming an increasingly dangerous proposition, continue to play the roles assigned to them by their exploiters: that of subject territories. The natives imitate the actions and ideology of the colonial powers. These no man's lands attract the disaffected of all cultures; self-realization for such individuals can only mean a knowledge of their own hollowness which induces extreme despair.

These are not novels which portray the tragic hero or an anti-utopia. Considered separately the horror they conjure is likely to be treated as an extreme situation. Together the two novels touch a core of conviction by presenting a complete world which is ordinary and actual. The horror becomes personal for the reader as it almost touches his skin.

These novels hold opposites in balance to show a suspended, animated, divided world which is stationary with hardly any movement, literal or literary. A slight change in the narrator's bias is noticeable in favour of a subjective reality which moves from 'I' to 'we.' In *Guerrillas* Roche says about Jane:

> She knew only what she was and what she had been born to; to this knowledge she was tethered: it was her stability, enabling her to adventure in security. Adventuring, she was indifferent, perhaps blind, to the contradiction between what she said and what she was so secure of being; and this indifference or blindness, this absence of the sense of the absurd, was part of her unassailability. (25)

Towards the end Jane redeems herself in the tenderness she shows towards Peter after he returns depressed by the radio interview with Meredith. And her last visit to Jimmy is a putting into action of her belief that he had been 'let down' by Peter. She must atone for this white man's betrayal of the "Nigger."

Salim's consistent emphasis on 'I' when the narrative begins in *A Bend in the River* can be interestingly contrasted with the account on the last two pages. The 'I' becomes 'we' and the final paragraph is a third person impersonal account which only reminds one of human experience because it describes purely sensory experiences. The structural and psychological balance between the subjective and objective, internal and external, is maintained by the narrator playing a dual role in order to achieve omniscience and verisimilitude. His awareness alternates between that of the actor and the observer. The significance of the chronological progression of the narratives is dissipated by the fact of stasis in subjective reality: for experience does not lead to decisive change. The haunting presence of the unacknowledged yet very real island and town is reduced by the unreal, peripheral yet solid outside world of London, South Africa, the Indian Ocean, Persia and Arabia. And ironically the journeys between the two keep them apart.

The narrators present, to the reader, a triple vision in these novels. There is the overall atmosphere of despair, there is the apparently smooth surface of routine in which societies function, where disturbance erupts as if without warning and there is the subliminal world of subjective reality which is aware of the other two worlds; but this third world has so taken over the personality that as an active member of society it has ceased to exist. It is here, in the subjective reality of individuals that the reader searches for and finds the genesis of despair. Formed by society, they inject their pessimism, anger, hate and inadequacy into their social situation, sealing off an enclosing world. Hollow at the core, if they move, their movement covers only a short distance between their existential anguish and the smooth surface of the material world. This movement between their two worlds provides relief for it suggests a measure of freedom, of having escaped from a trap, as well as anguish for it denies the stability of a resting place.

The author, Naipaul, sees those who do not move as the doomed though they themselves are unaware of their danger:

But tranquillity recedes. The barracoon is overcrowded; the escape routes are closed. The people are disaffected and have no sense of danger.[*]

The wholly subjective worlds of these novels portray a vision of despair which, like the haze created by the intense heat of *Guerrillas* or the choking sensation caused by the water hyacinths in the river, entrapping man's awareness, lies just below the surface of sensitive life today and which no thinking man who turns inwards, in disgust from mindless living, can avoid. It is compounded by the fact that it cannot be blamed on any single cause; there is no resolution to it nor escape from it. However, the narrator simultaneously suggests, in a low key, certain situations which provide air-vents to dissipate the accumulating sensation of violence. There is no 'leap in the dark' to a higher order of living as a permanent answer to existential anguish; no angelic state of permanent joy is suggested. There is no apocalyptic vision and nothing new enters to radically alter the structure of the world. The routes away from despair are age-old and much-travelled-pleasure and communion. The newness is in a fresh revelation to the protagonist of what he took for granted as commonplace. Jimmy is trapped by his despair, feeling 'alone and unloved,' enough to wish for death.

> The corridor of time is now a room of mirrors, it just shows me forever picking myself up, and this time I want them to count me out. (227)

Yet he is grateful enough to Marge for having made him 'a man' to write what he thinks is his last letter to her. In this letter, expressing his love for Bryant, he finally realizes the latter's hold on him and offers Jane as a sacrifice to appease him. He realizes his power in the island when Peter tells him over the phone that he is leaving for London and leaving Jimmy alone and untouched though he is the murderer of Jane, Jimmy has regained a 'fix on reality' through perverted love and a destructive power. It is a frightening picture of the escape routes a despairing man will take. Marie Therese, the loyal wife and mother, representing the centre of stability on the Ridge, leaves her husband and home to travel only a short distance, literally and literarily, to become the mistress of a civil servant:

> Now, to many people on the Ridge, his news was like a double confirmation of the instability in which they all knew they lived. (124)

Marie Therese's despair to death is expressed through Jane's vision as she hears Harry express his views about music--it should be permitted only in jail and in Peter's head! He has never tapped his feet to music! Jane says she knows why his wife left him. 'Having a good time' is her answer to Harry's smothering respectability.

Ferdinand's act of friendship towards Salim in warning him to leave the town before it is 'too late' is contrasted with the latter's betrayal of Metty in leaving him behind. This gesture of friendship, in gratitude for past patronage, redeems Salim to the ordinary social world of marriage and business. Ferdinand's despair at having no future, no escape, is alleviated by the temporary exercise of power to benefit a friend and the fact that his mother, having gone back to the bush, is someone he can fall back on.

The primarily social as well as the personal aspects of the same subjective reality are projected through the differing omniscient visions of the narrators of *Guerrillas* and *A Bend in the River*. In the former objectivity is achieved by the narrator in a Joycean manner, refining himself out of existence, and in the latter by identifying his consciousness with that of the autobiographer, Salim. He is a reflective, knowledgeable person in search of experience who encompasses within his vision as much of the wider world as is consistent with his character. He examines his world of adventure and romance in the language of trade, being the son of a business family.

All the themes of *Guerrillas* which build up a picture of despair and social breakdown are dramatized by the dual consciousness of the narrator: alienation from the land, from society and from self--from the important world. It dramatizes not only the static drifting society of the idle and the inactive (no one is seen working for a living--they have no cause for which to fight!) ironically claiming to be doers and saviours, but it also becomes a dialogue between the personal past and present as each character examines and exposes himself or the other. (It takes a public riot, bombings, burnings, acts of sabotage or deep personal injury to activate them only to realize that they are lagging far behind the reality of life on the island). Each one sees himself as a wasted potential, no one more so than Jimmy. His character is most rounded through his writings which enlarge on his fantasies regarding himself; here he exp .ses

129

his present despair most truthfully as he realizes the distance between the imagined and the actual self. Nobody knows him as well as the reader. To his society he remains an unknown quantity which adds glamour and substance to his reputed personality.

The narrator narrates in his dual capacity without disturbing the smoothness of the narrative by subtle transitions from one role to the other. He is the third person omniscient narrator who describes with equal sympathy the two overtly conflicting social groups of disaffected people: the whites versus the coloureds, the expatriates versus the locals, the Ridge versus the Grange. Within these there are various shades and transitions of loyalties to people and ideas as well as defections from one to the other. He further describes the individual actions and dialogues, the landscape and the plot of the story sustaining unity from beginning to end through the use of precise and unemotional language and by emphasizing actuality through repeated description of the physical geography of the island:

> AFTER LUNCH Jane and Roche left their house on the Ridge to drive to Thrushcross Grange. They drove down to the hot city at the foot of the hills, and then across the city to the sea-road, through thoroughfares daubed with slogans: 'Basic Black', 'Don't Vote,' 'Birth Control is a Plot Against the Negro Race.'
> The openness didn't last for long. Villages had become supurbs. . . .
> Traffic was heavy in this area of factories. But the land still showed its recent pastoral history. (9-10)

And again towards the end of the novel:

> And then he was on the highway, locked in the afternoon traffic, and he was being taken past all the stations of that familiar drive. . . . The junked cars beside the road; the country settlements; the burning rubbish dump, lorries and people amid the smoke and the miniature hills of confetti-like refuse

... the bauxite pall; the hot, squalling afternoon city, melting tar, honking buses and taxis and enraged, sweating cyclists. (250)

The narrator is also the consciousness of each of his characters not only as they speak silently to themselves or in dialogue, using speech consistent with their personalities and role-playing, but also when the landscape becomes emotionally tinged. Certain third person descriptions of the landscape are not neutral but definitely the vision of one or other of the characters. The transition from one to the other is very neat so that the margin between the actual and the emotional, the character and his narrator is very fine. Thus a society of unique individuals is created, for we see them in interaction with others and their landscape: influencing and being influenced, communicating their fears and receiving the emotional tensions of others, criticizing and being criticized. They see themselves and we see them gradually being reduced, shrinking into themselves. We see a brittle society breaking up, the surface cracking to reveal the depths of individual despair.

The description of Jimmy's house on Jane's and Roche's first visit is by the omniscient narrator. It is exact and reflects the personality of Jimmy as the narrator wishes us to see him:

Sunlight struck full on the terrazzo porch, and the sitting-room caught the glare. A square of English carpet, electric-blue with splashes of black and yellow, almost cover the floor. ... A blue-tinted glass vase held three switches of bougainvillea. It was a room without disorder; it had obviously been prepared for this visit.

Jane says, "But it's like being in England." (24)

On the third visit we see the same room through Jane's eyes and are repulsed for the description is invested by her fears and self-disgust.

He walked into the living room and Jane followed him. She saw again the electric-blue carpet with the black and yellow

131

splashes; . . .

Roche opened the door into the kitchen; and the sight and smell of dirty plates, stale food going bad in the heat, strange food, further unsettled her. She thought: I feel like screaming. The thought came to her as words alone; but within herself she began to stimulate an imaginary scream. (163-64)

The oblong windows showed a colourless sky. But Jane had a sense now of more than heat; she had a sense of desolation. (17)

The first sentence in the narrator's idiom transits to Jane's almost hysterical emotionalism in the second:

They came to the main square, once an area of trees and asphalted walks, now full of parked motorcars and rough wooden stalls. . . . The sea, when they came to it, gave no feeling of air and lightness: the fine red powder of bauxite, sheds of corroded corrugated iron, the reek of the burning rubbish dump: everything here, hillside, forest, sea, mangrove, turned to slum. (75)

The first part of the paragraph is the narrator's awareness of the landscape which in the later half represents Jane's and Roche's combined sensibilities.

Right through the novel there is this movement between the consciousness of the narrator and his characters creating a surface unity but revealing its thinness and vulnerability as it succumbs to the passions of the inhabitants of the land. Through this contrasting vision the narrator builds up the subjective reality of a society out of sympathy with the land which sustains it and therefore truly free-floating and free-wheeling in spite of all its professions of loyalty. We are shown a 'way of life' whose clutches the best-intentioned cannot escape for it spreads its vicious tentacles of pseudo-freedom and entraps by distorting as the haze of heat over the island.

The various subjective realities of the expatriate society of the Ridge, through whose eyes we see the town and the Grange, provide

132

the outsiders's view of third world chaos, disorder and subhuman existence. Theirs is the despair of having come as messengers of goodwill to uplift and present a new hope on behalf of the western world only to find that they are at the mercy of 'beasts' and their own similar hungers. Jimmy's, and indirectly Bryant's, consciousness pervades the novel from beginning to end. However, we see that this frightful image of the third world is partly a consequence of this society itself or what it represents: the exploiters who have used Jimmy and taken advantage of his credulity to serve their own ends.

In *Guerrillas* we see a thoroughly contemporary materialistic society, without faith, ideas or ideals and no idea of itself. Through Jimmy's writings is projected the negative impact of this society on the intelligence and energy of simpler people. In reverse we become aware of the repercussion on society of a single, disaffected, intelligent consciousness which becomes fertile ground for rebel leadership and gangster politics--the ground for revolution without a programme or guerrilla warfare without a cause. Ironically, this is stemmed, for the time being, by the very game the foreigners play: the game of self-analysis. Jimmy has become imbued with the spirit of self-examination and realizes that all, including himself, is "rotten meat," and the will to fight leaves him.

The significance of *A Bend in the River* can be better understood if the two social situations are contrasted. In these two novels the narrator comes to grips with the psychological reality of the association between the colonial west and the colonized third world. Evoked subjectively with an ample expression of moods, passions, sentiments and emotions, they leave a deep impression of the far-reaching and almost lasting damage done to the third world psyche. The extent of this injury is revealed through the metaphor of distances and journeys. The island of *Guerrillas*, almost exhausted of its economic potential, its human potential distorted through misuse, is a convenient junkyard for the discarded machines and unwanted men of the west. The decay spreads so that the remnants of island respectability and colonial order are affected adversely. They prepare for flight, becoming, ironically, like the birds of passage Peter and Jane, who occupy an ambiguous social

133

position on the Ridge; the break-up of their relationship is one of the themes of the novel. The Grandlieus sink into unimportance and the de Tunjas have already made a nest for themselves in Canada. Those who must stay, like Stephen's mother, retreat into superstitious religion, self-glorifying, waiting for Africa's hour of glory as prophesied. One realizes that these are the true expatriates whereas the emotional orientation of Peter and Jane, unanchored souls, makes their sensibilities akin to those of Jimmy and Bryant: the true natives.

In *A Bend in the River* the central African state becomes a junkyard for different reasons though its inhabitants are also out of sympathy with the land. Though exploited, its wealth, material and manpower, is far from exhausted. It is choked by its own lushness and richness and the inability of its people to defend themselves leave alone meet the challenges of the modern world. The fatalistic outlook of the past, 'it will go on,' 'the town will rise again,' alters into an equally unsatisfactory vision of an Africa which is an abstraction. Neither yield a social vision or lead to responsible action. In this junkyard of obsolete and irrelevant ideas adventurers like Raymond and the Big Man, literally and literarily, search for ivory at great risk to their lives. It will go on but it will never be important! Ironically, Raymond, trying to modernize the state, without comprehension of its needs and its potential, with imported ideas, conducting research and writing books on the tribes, is out of sympathy with the land. Later Salim discovers that much of the research has been based on newspaper cuttings! Yvette is more affected by the rebuff she receives from the President, more involved in her affair with Salim, more concerned with her husband's future and his present position, than in getting to know the land in which she lives. Similarly Salim, Mahesh and Shobha, Noiman, Nazruddin, all outsiders though not expatriates, feel no links with the town and make no efforts to establish them. For these people the town is an antagonist which must be mastered and enslaved. They measure their cunning and wit against its trade potential in order to make money, banked abroad, out of its disorder. If one did not see their weaknesses and desires encom-

134

passed by some idea of self and society one would be inclined to consider them more rapacious than the society of *Guerrillas*.

Zabeth, rooted in her tribal ways, observant and intelligent, is the only one who experiences the existential agony of the land, and impotent, retreats into the bush. Speaking about her Salim says,

> She didn't see the photograph as a photograph; she didn't *interpret* distance and perspective. She was concerned with the *actual* space occupied in the printed picture by different figures. . . . With local people the President was always presented as a towering figure.
>
> 'He is killing those men, Salim. They are screaming inside, and he knows they're screaming. And you know, Salim, that isn't a fetish he's got there. It's nothing.' (241)

The sons of the soil, Ferdinand and the boys at the lyceé, reveal the germs of growing disaffection when they question the white man's religion, culture and education which has transformed their former free life in the bush into the slavery of house boys in 'proper' uniforms or into military fodder for warring leaders. They think seriously about the future of Africa but as Salim and Indar realize they are without the intellectual equipment which will translate their ideas into action. Newly-acquired borrowed thoughts and borrowed words sink into ideas of self-importance. Their world of faith is powerless against the faithless white world, for they still revert to magic which, though it can exorcise spirits, cannot eject colonizers out of their state. Only the slow process of education, which will take a long time to cover the distance to the West, provides some hope. And the possibility of catching up seems remote. Theirs is not a social vision in the contemporary sense of a society of responsible individual members. They serve in small, insufficient ways the members of their immediate community.

The Western world had accentuated the tribal idea of 'might is right' so that Zabeth and others whose past world has been organized on the principle of 'hunter' and 'hunted,' accepted it as a more powerful tribe. Exploitation was part of African realism and they did not yet have an idea of nationhood. They do not experience the racial resentment of the American negro. Their despair is more immediate: how to save their skins against inevitable oppression. But traditional routes are closing up. Zabeth can return to the bush for she has not travelled far--only between the village and the town-- though perceptually she is far ahead of the others. Ferdinand, trapped by the white man's culture and idea of Self, by notions of duty to a non-existent state, as commissioner, must stay. He cannot take the routes open to the 'outsiders' who have nothing to lose by leaving. Ferdinand's is the despair that faces death and he is the new man of Africa!

So the problem of distances, ironically, converges into the idea of a single despairing world. Everywhere Salim goes is the same place. London is another town on a bend in the river, another junkyard for refugees living in a world without ideas:

> But the Europe I had come to--and knew from the outset I was coming to--was neither the old Europe nor the new. It was something shrunken and mean and forbidding. . . . Of this Europe I could form no mental picture. But it was there in London; it couldn't be missed; and there was no mystery. The effect of those little stalls, booths, kiosks and choked grocery shops--run by people like myself--was indeed of people who had squashed themselves in. They traded in the middle of London as they had traded in the middle of Africa. The goods travelled a shorter distance, but the relationship of the trader to his goods remained the same. . . . They were cut off from the life of the great city where they had come to live, and I wondered about the pointlessness of their own hard life, the pointlessness of their difficult journey. (247)

The greatest distance for the characters of this novel is between the past and the present. And their world is divided between those who trample on the past to live successfully in the present, among whom Nazruddin and Indar count themselves till they meet with more refined examples of indifference and self-

136

centred opportunism in the U.S.A., and people like Salim, whom the world passes by. For such people the move into the present is painful and slow as they still hold on to social ideals of the past: justice, fair-dealing, courtesy and duty. The relativity of life associated with the metaphor of the journey is hence stressed not only through the spatial dimension as distance and place but also through the time dimension as a matter of speed.

The frightful vision of an asocial conglomeration of peoples at the town on the bend in the river, grabbing and running, as one more third world reality, is created through Salim's autobiographical, reflective and meditative narrative. The language is poetic and emotive. The landscape alters according to his mood and company. He has the quality of empathy which enables him to see himself and others as well as the landscape through other people's eyes. This capacity assures critical self-knowledge without reducing the emotive power of the experience. One sees the different sources for the same feeling of despair and fear the hunted experience. And so the total single mood of the novel is extended to its limits. One sees the historical and imaginative world reduced as Salim is repeatedly disillusioned in himself and in others. The only people who support his self-esteem while driving home his failure in a world of ideas and ideals are Zabeth and Ferdinand. Salim's double vision--the sublime and the ridiculous--is the basis of a growing personal reality as much as its undoing, for it makes him doubt the sincerity of his experience; indeed he remains a stranger to existenz/the land.

The hyacinths of the river, floating on: during the days of the rebellion they had spoken of blood; on heavy afternoons of heat and glitter they had spoken of experience without savour; white is moonlight, they had matched the mood of a particular evening. Now, lilac on bright green, they spoke of something over, other people moving on. (170)

My own nervousness was soothed; my mood was buoyant--I would leave the steamer with Yvette.

The light was the light of the very early afternoon--everything stoked up, the blaze got truly going, but with a hint

137

of the blaze about to consume itself. The river glittered, muddy water turned to white and gold. . . . Sometimes, when a dugout crossed a patch of glitter, the occupants were all silhouetted against the glitter . . . so that for a while they were like comic figures in a cartoon strip, engaged on some quite ridiculous journey. (178)

This could be a perception of the adventure he is about to embark upon with Yvette. His perception of the actuality of the Domain is heightened and distorted by his awareness of Indar's and Nazruddin's views of it and his own uncertainty relating to Yvette:

Nazruddin's old words came to me. This is nothing. This is just bush! But my alarm wasn't like Nazruddin's. It had nothing to do with my business prospects . . . and my thoughts were of Yvette and her life on the Domain. Not Europe in Africa, as it had seemed to me, when Indar was there. Only a life in the bush. And my fear was at once the fear of failing with her, being left with nothing, and the fear of the consequences of success. (186)

This empathy with others and this extensive vision, however imperfect, covering wide historical periods and geographical areas, of varied and opposite cultures is a natural feature of Salim's personality brought up as he has been in the multi-cultural and multi-layered social environment of the east coast. His sources of information vary from pictures on stamps, gossip and beliefs of family slaves, observation of life in the compound, family history passed down and the conversations of Nazruddin and Indar both of whom are a strange mixture of Hindu, Muslim and European thought and culture. Added to this is his education at the 'local English-language college' and the various general knowledge and science magazines he contributes to in the town. But early he realizes the insufficiency at the core of his personality and decides that

To stay with my community, to pretend that I had simply to travel along with them, was to be taken with them to destruction. I could be master of my fate only if I stood alone. (26)

Salim has grown up with ideas of societal and social reality which have no base in personal experience. And his failing is also the failing of his society. His secure childhood gives him an expansive personality itching for adventure and success. His too secure future, planned and organized by his elders, instigates him into rebel action given the necessary encouragement by Nazruddin. In this way the narrator preserves the unity of the narrative, literal and literary, to give us a multi-level picture of the horror, chaos and disorder of the town.

The idiom is consistently Salim's, its alteration of tone and texture coinciding with the growth of his awareness. He himself admits that contact with Yvette has changed his manner of seeing and expressing. The narrator does not intrude, comment or present any contrary evidence to that of Salim. All important events and personalities are seen, analysed, categorized and philosophized by him alone. This conjunction of action and thought, stated in the beginning by Salim himself as a childhood habit, characterizes the movement of the narrative giving it coherence, unity and a sense of purpose as well as rhythm. It also enacts Salim's own final act of withdrawal from the world in shame and self-castigation. Unreflected, impulsive action leads to his search for adventure as reflection leads to withdrawal and inaction. Investing the world with his own self has led to pain. Now he wishes to see the world uninvested with the self and so his double vision, a childhood trait, matures. It explains pain and despair but discourages creative participation. All the richness of his experience has resulted only in self-doubt and like Jimmy, he becomes incapable of acting and is only acted upon. Yet through this disturbing change is visible the truth of Ralph Singh's comment that personality, like the narrative, is 'one and indivisible.'

The narrator thus refines himself away by depicting a small world as the largest reality of Salim. Naipaul, by arbitrarily dividing the narrative--disturbing its flow--into sections, titled after significant events, a place which represents a contemporary cultural complex and an important man whose dominance in contemporary politics cannot be overlooked--presents Salim's despair as partially illusory and self-created. These events, places and people have remained unreal, being only marginally present in Salim's consciousness, never becoming a contrary balancing reality. By placing Salim's world in the context of one he had ignored, Naipaul creates the ironic context. Salim's world, multiple though it is, is viewed by him in its sameness not its difference, in its ultimate not its relative value. For all his seeming sophistication he remains the 'island innocent.' Distanced, the despair would have been less pervasive for he would have been conscious of material reality as subject to a particular time and place.

To Salim, Indar represents the contrary vision, something to aspire to, something that makes him feel small. But from Kareisha he learns that Indar, like any other 'innocent' from the third world made a faith out of ideas and tried to live up to it only to fail. Treated like an outsider, a superfluous person, by the West, he thinks of going home. Ultimately he has returned to where he began, seeking comfort in old ways of feeling, living a truly invisible life, not wanted where he was and having trampled on his past, having no place to return to:

> That illumination I held on to, about the unity of experience and the illusion of pain, was part of the same way of feeling. We fell into it--people like Indar and myself--because it was the basis of our old way of life. But I had rejected that way of life--and just in time. . . . There could be no going back; there was nothing to go back to. We had become what the world outside had made us; we had to live in the world as it existed. The younger Indar was wiser. (261-62)

The narrator of *Guerrillas* presents dramatic external evidence of the necessary links between society and the individual. The narrator of *A Bend in the River* submerges us immediately into the personal reality of Salim where we see these links being broken, forged and reforged continually as he orients himself to the present, accompanied by all the horror that unbearable pain, whether real or imagined, arouses. Salim, like Jimmy, is the victim of society, but for different reasons. We see him struggling to free himself from the grip of a meaningless society which subsists on archaic ideas through which contemporary existence continues to be viewed and lived, removed from present reality and an assumed past. Like the hunter he struggles through the jungle of the historical past, travelling backwards in time reversing the route the slaves took from the centre to the coast of Africa. Simultaneously in his ancestor's otherwise gory history of slave trade he discovers the sources of adventure, power and romance. He journeys through these imaginatively elevating regions in his stay in the town which remains unreal because unknown by him and with which he develops no real sympathy. It is this failure of sympathy with the land the present which, as the antagonist and the more powerful of the two, strips him of historical and imaginative life to leave him to face his own hollowness and vulnerability, dependent on others for his survival. His life he owes to Ferdinand. His bruised and battered dignity is entrusted to Nazruddin and Kareisha to be restored. Though he has travelled far, literally and literarily, he has moved only a short distance, seemingly in a circle, back to the stability of an inherited order he had tried to escape when he left the coast: back to the security of an arranged marriage and a business partnership with Nazruddin, secure in his personal manhood having discarded all his acquired notions and liabilities as he leaves the town finally on his outward journey. His future with Kareisha promises romance as he has developed a personal relationship with her and he is now Nazruddin's equal whom all his life he has viewed as a superior.

And so the novel points up degree of despair measured by the sense of closeness or distance to 'a home.' It shows varying degrees of closure to the outside life and varying routes of escape. It points up the knowledge that Salim ultimately arrives at--that society and individual sink or swim together. The last passage of the novel, in which unknown and unrelated to any other member of the steamer's

141

community Salim records his observations in the second and third persons, indicates this understanding.

Naipaul presents to us young people with all the promise of a fulfilling creative life turning sour for, in whichever direction they turn, they discover their dreams to be insubstan.ial. In turning away they broke their connections with a known though unrealized world; now there is no social reference and therefore there is no cause to fight for. Continued existential fear has destroyed their will, and has led to the self-destroying security of habitual behaviour.

In these two novels Naipaul has meditated on the meaning of existential despair in terms of the third world. Existential despair without the 'leap of faith' has been the lot of third world people who have been influenced by the pseudo-existentialist living which characterizes the marginal men of the West, who, rejects from their own society, set up their flags in remote regions among the 'innocents' of simple cultures. The colonizer, along with handing over political power to the colonized has handed over his despair with it without the means of retreat assured to the secure of the world.

He shows it in its most ugly form in situations where the third and first world meet deliberately or accidentally to exploit each other, the one culturally and the other economically. This coming together for mutual gain does not constitute a society. However, material failure can be borne, but cultural failure, implying a spiritual loss, is disastrous as is witnessed in the case of Indar, Ferdinand and Salim. Culture cannot be exploited, it can only be cultivated. By the time this lesson comes home it is too late. Besides there seems to be a fundamental opposition between the cultivation of money and the cultivation of culture. Money triumphs. For without it a borrowed culture is not possible. So Salim, neglecting money to pursue culture under Yvette's tutelage, ends up a complete failure. This is the despairing picture of contemporary third world values. For the culture that is one's own subsumes within it the concepts of money-making. Nazruddin finally perceives:

The trouble with people like us, running about the world with money to hide, is that we are good about business only in our own places. (253)

But trying to purchase another's culture with your own assets is not feasible. This is what Indar learns in the house of the American who treated him like an equal. Indar, staying in cheap hotels, feels used, treated as a toy, when he enters the opulent house of his patron and realizes that it is the latter's wealth which enables him to play the role of an equal.

Naipaul also shows the closing up of routes to dignity. Disaffected societies promising illusory power and freedom are no alternative to the stagnating sterility of tradition-bound societies.or those whose wheels run smoothly on economic prosperity. Each leads to a kind of despair and death-wish. To keep alive and free is to keep moving.

In these novels Naipaul is as interested in portraying the psychological reality of the thiru world at a particular historical moment as in examining critically the bias of the 'objective' narrator. The relationship between Naipaul and the narrator is that of the artist with his creature. The narrator can assume many roles depending on his intentions but underlying these roles is Naipaul's vision of the world.

Naipaul creates a further distinction between the artist as artist and the artist as man. Irony and ambiguity characterize the artist's grasp of the world but for Naipaul himself certain philosophical issues are very clear. In his novels the philosophical and artistic issues coincide so that style and matter mutually reflect the significance of his fiction.

Naipaul's world functions on the principles of relativity and balance. Objective/subjective, real/unreal, rational/imaginative, truth/fiction, time/place, art/existenz, literal/literary, protagonist/ narrator, artist/man, first world/third world, may meet, merge and become indistinguishable but can never attain the wholeness of the 'one and indivisible.' Hence Naipaul's metaphors never attain to symbolism.

143

The narrator travelling self-consciously only in one direction loses his grip on the other. He will end up as the 'nothing' that is an abstraction or become superimposed on the personality of his protagonist. The narrator, in trying to give a coherent view of the world through a consistent point of view, converts the living world into an artefact. For it is only in the narrative that the narrator and audience can approach oneness. A book can approximate life but can never become it. The narrator therefore is only one aspect of the artist's personality pursuing itself and the world to logical conclusions. Naipual creates his fiction through the juxtaposition of the rational and the irrational man--the narrator and the protagonist respectively--each viewing the world in a particular way. He implies an existent opposition between the feeling, reflecting and acting man.

Therefore the artist as man is removed from the artist as such for the acting man can never be wholly subsumed under the reflective, meditative and creative faculty. The artist influencing and being influenced by the man finds it hard if not impossible to distinguish between the actual and the imagined reality. In these circumstances Naipaul asserts the value of rational living. It provides the groundwork for order and distance necessary to the artist, who creates out of pain and disillusionment controlled.

This human and artistic need for order makes judgment a basic quality of being human. To that extent every man is an artist. Beneath the surface of objective art criticism is implicit in the choice of events, characters, language, technique and style. Objective narration is the most subjective account of the narrator's mind. The objective narrator, by avoiding overt judgment, though in tune with the contemporary reality of the world of man and of art, is objective only at the expense of a full expression of his self and his vision.

Naipaul suggests that all art is subjective. It is one man's experience of the world. His work presents the ordering of one man's world. A work of art can never be converted into a philosophical system. And the artist has constantly to contend with his need for order and his fear of its threat to his psyche implicit in the

144

concept of order.

NOTES

1. *The Mimic Men*, p. 52.
2. V.S. Naipaul, *Guerrillas* (Harmondsworth: Penguin, 1977), p. 104.
3. V.S. Naipaul, *A Bend in the River* (Delhi: Clarion Books, 1980), p. 291.
4. *Ibid.*, p. 30.
5. V.S. Naipaul, *The Return of Eva Peron with the Killings in Trinidad* (London: Andre Deutsch, 1980), p. 212.
6. *The Overcrowded Barracoon and Other Articles*, p. 309.

In a Free State:
Into the Fourth Dimension

In the novels so far studied Naipaul has followed recognizable patterns of the tradition of the novel, staying close to the novel of sensibility. He has regulated the distance between the protagonist, narrator, author and reader to ensure that the dominant vision of each novel is that of the narrator, leaving the novels open-ended. Though there are dramatic and literary resolutions in the lives of the protagonist and the narrator, respectively, in each novel--the latter arriving at a centre of stillness, however temporary. Naipaul, by depicting the narrator as the controlling agent of the novel, suggests other stories with different narrators and different endings. However, even though it is the narrator's vision and pain which is prominent it is the protagonist's existential reality that dominates the story, the narrator/author being present by implication or intrusively and the artist's vision being a critical assumption of the reader based on the dramatic/psychological structure of the novel.

Juxtaposing conflicting political, social and personal realities as the differing existential situations in the lives of the narrator and the protagonist, the author conveys his overall vision of a fragmented world in which individuals and societies are trapped in their own unreal realities, meeting Reality only tangentially. For the artist it is a painful experience of alienation as well as a challenge to his vision and art to project a sense of possibility, a sense of 'home' and a harmonious world order from an awareness of fracture, isolation, lack of community and finally total disorder.

In a Free State makes a statement about the relationship between experience, vision and art as a third world reality. The distance between these aspects of life is regulated by the capacity and circumstances of the concerned individual. It is therefore as

146

much a description and a vision of external expatriate reality as a pictorial projection of the working of the artist's mind and his use of materials and techniques: of the genesis of the novel. These are complementary processes: the novel grows out of the experiences of life as well as of the processes of art. The experience of expatriation is seen as a common feature of life today. Today, as never before, the third world has become aware of its anonymity and unimportance which is as much a consequence of its historical past as of undeniable contemporary political, social and economic pressures. In an increasingly shrinking, industrialized and auto-mated world as more and more individuals and peoples begin to feel unnecessary and obsolete the struggle for survival acquires greater urgency and obstinacy. Through a work of art the anonymous mass man achieves an identity, affirmation and individuality. The artist focuses his attention on the real world forcing people, who are becoming increasingly alienated from it, as they seek release from present tensions by living in the past or future, to pay attention to it. The novel no longer represents a slice of life but becomes an activating agent in the development and fulfilment of man's desire to achieve selfhood.

Therefore, in this novel, the relationship between the protagonist, the narrator and the author is of no consequence for the vision projected is a single one; the awareness of the protagonist growing into that of the narrator and the artist. The emphasis is as much on the quality of the vision as on its use as a means for describing a single developing awareness. One sees the emergence of the personality of the narrator as artist in his own right, not used by the author to project his own ironic vision. The narrator projects his own reality as the protagonist and the artist. He juxtaposes his experience with accounts of varied third world personalities who, though important to themselves, can be seen as typical, common and general, for these are people controlled by their circumstances. He parenthesizes these three accounts between extracts from his journal giving the unquestionable impression that these accounts have significance only in relation to the narrator's experience/vision. He is protagonist/narrator in the journal extracts and author/

narrator in the three stories.

Unlike the earlier narrators he visualizes the consciousness of the protagonist as part of his own particular awareness. Santosh's loss of an ideal self, Dayo's brother's loss of a complete love and Bobby's sense of a loss of a supporting environment, all as a consequence of a growth in knowledge through disillusioning interaction with reality, reflect analogously the lonely tramp at odds with his environment deeply conscious of his vulnerability. The tramp is the only character with whom the narrator empathizes. Every character in the book seeks by self-exposure through narration to fill in the void and thus repossess the self and the world. The protagonist calls a halt to his despair and the narrator achieves status as an artist. His journal, descriptive, reflective and meditative, focussing on a community of exposed, vulnerable people, leads to and becomes part of the novel.

It is the distinct function of the narrator to create the contingent world as objectively as possible. He is a craftsman, very much a part of the world he creates. The needs of narration--logic, precision, clarity and verisimilitude--of necessity restrict the narrative to the reality of the narrator and therefore bias cannot altogether be eliminated. The artist rises above him to present the ambiguity, variety and palpability of a flexible reality in a state of flux which alters the moment it is asserted. The artist uses the narrator to arrest one such moment in all its multiplicity to give an overall vision of contemporary man: his failures, successes and possibilities.

Naipaul's vision is not an eternal truth about life, death or love or other universal constants arrived at intuitively. It is a moment of individual existential despair which extends its jaundiced understanding to cover the world. This despair illuminates a moment of time before it becomes history. The narrator builds up an understanding of this despair. It is revealed as a consequence of subconscious rational processes at work long before the moment of its emergence to consciousness. The actions of Santosh, Dayo's brother, Bobby and the tramp are ordered by a particular logic even though it leads to disorder, break-up and anguish. Illumination comes to each of them only through a retracing of their lives, juxtaposing time present and time past. Though this understanding leads to a reduction of life it provides them with a hold on it by establishing a sense of continuity in an otherwise fragmented existence. Naipaul is not a pessimist though his vision is such. A vision attained through rational processes, conscious or subconscious, implies a search for possibilities measured against and defined by actualities.

This fullness of vision is created through projecting, by implication, a wider world and placing the narrator's world in it creating ironic tensions. Naipaul achieves this through the metaphorical vibrations set up by the titles of his novels: *The Mystic Masseur, The Mimic Men, A House for Mr. Biswas, A Bend in the River, Guerrillas* and *In a Free State;* by the use of epilogues and prologues as in *A House for Mr. Biswas* and *In a Free State,* epigram in the *Guerrillas* and section headings as in *A Bend in the River.* The relationship between the narrator and the artist is comparable to the relationship between a world of order and that of mystery, between one of reason and that of intuitive awareness. Naipaul presents these not only as contrary but also as complementary awarenesses, the presence of the one implying that of the other.

In a Free State is a composite of first person reporting of events experienced by the narrator and made available to the reader as pages from his journal and three fictive accounts. The first two are in the stream-of-consciousness mode. The third is a dramatic, third person account with emphasis on chronological detailing of the journey by car as Bobby's growth in awareness as he travels with Linda through 'no man's land.' One sees the modern intellectual sensibility unable to be totally involved as experience is accompanied by simultaneous analysis of it. This exterior structure of the book, so evidently composed of disparate items, is loosely held together thematically by the latent relationship between absurdity and freedom, and structurally through the deliberate use by the narrator of his journalistic nonfictional accounts as parentheses for the fiction.

The surface structure then consists of five episodes. Each episode is in itself a complete story with a narrator, a protagonist, an action, a resolution, a mood and a vision. Each story reflects a total situation in its own context but a partial one in that of the novel. As analogues for the narrator's experience, unhesitatingly depicted in the prologue and the epilogue, they build up a novel of sensibility with emphasis on mood and subjectivity. They reflect a latent single vision whose genesis is in the experience of existential futility of the narrator while defending the dignity of the Arab urchin against the Italian tourist who baits the hungry child with food as a form of amusement in the rest house at Luxor. His personal frustration illuminates a particular truth about his contingent world: neither the oppressor nor the oppressed have a concept of personal and human dignity. It is a remnant of the past in the narrator's own personality which makes his action a wasted gesture:

> Perhaps that had been the only pure time, at the beginning, when the ancient artist, knowing no other land, had learned to look at his own and had seen it as complete. But it was hard, travelling back to Cairo, looking with my stranger's eye at the fields and the people who worked in them, the dusty downs, the agitated peasant crowds at railway stations, it was hard to believe that there had been such innocence. Perhaps that vision of the land, in which the Nile was only water, a blue-green chevron, had always been a fabrication, a cause for yearning, something for the tomb.[1]

The surface structure directs the attention of the reader to the narrator's subjective world, his dilemmas and his vision as a man and artist. It also presents the narrator's wide and varied experience of the world. Geographically it covers the important world: Bombay/Washington, Trinidad/London, African Reality (actual and imagined, black and white) and Cairo and its environs. Within this important world of business and power politics the narrator views a cross section of contemporary humanity in the grip of contemporary culture in which power and money are the criterion of importance. The panorama ranges from the most deprived and dispossessed, the third world's third world--people like Santosh, Dayo's

150

brother, Arab urchins, Egyptian soldiers returning defeated from Sinai, Greek refugees, the tramp--at one end, to the materially sound and secure people like Bobby and Linda, the Lebanese businessman, the American and European tourists and sons of affluent Egyptians studying abroad. An ironic touch is added by the inclusion of the comfortably well-off Communist Chinese Circus at Luxor, distributing gifts, handshakes, money, medals and picture postcards of Chinese peonies--one empire replacing another. The rich and the poor can never meet though separated only by the distance of a deck on the steamer! Ironically, as the narration proceeds, the important aggressive world recedes and the subjective reality of the unimportant emerges as the significant fact of each story. Washington, London and the African State become less than meaningful when Santosh is faced with the powerful reality of his body and his mortality, Dayo's brother with the insubstantiality of his all-embracing love for Dayo, and Bobby, the colonial administrator, with the insecurity of the compound!

The narrator hence presents contemporary reality, the 'thing in itself' as a vast 'no man's land' in which those who grab, or scavenge or indulge themselves possess the original freedom of Alexander or Crusoe who to themselves are the only living realities in the world. This world is indifferent, if not hostile, to the subjective reality of the sensitive, reflective third world man who in his own orderly and imaginative fashion seeks to possess the world. Simultaneously the narrator also presents an emphatic image of the protagonist of each episode, literally and literarily in a 'free state,' detached from contingency as a result of a destructive encounter with reality.

In placing the 'free' world and the 'free' protagonist side by side, the depth of the latter's disillusionment is presented. The freedom of the upper deck of the steamer and the tourist rest house at Luxor, viewed from a distance, is the one aspired to and is also partially achieved by Santosh, Dayo's brother and Bobby. However, for these 'island innocents' the distance coalesces security with success. Only as they approach it do they realize the antithetical nature of these two realities. For with success life for these people has come to a standstill. In order to arrive they moved away from a 'home' but having arrived they do not 'belong' and so are stranded. But paradoxically, like a gift from the gods, their loss becomes the condition for their growth in self-awareness bringing with it the freedom of vision and perspective. Their sense of individuality, of subjective apartness from the world, may be painful but at least it combines the conditions of 'home' with those of freedom.

In Naipaul's fiction the greatest traps to self-expression are well-defined social systems; the greatest freedoms can be practised only in situations which represent no man's territory. The maximum aggression and the greatest growth in self-awareness occurs when contingent reality, in losing its contours, loosens its grips on man.

The narrator develops the multiple metaphorical implications of a 'free state' only by releasing settings from geographical, historical or social definition; here people form groups through chance, proximity or immediate purpose, without any deep `ties that bind.' We see people for whom the security of a 'room,' a 'home,' a 'flat' or a 'hideout' is beyond comprehension, for they are the secure of the earth, alongside people who have just lost that security. Their loss is so great that the centre of gravity shifts from the future to the past as something they can cling to. The present remains in danger of non-existence. It is the narrator who makes the present existent by recording the faint thrusts individuals make to assert their presence, to leave a mark on the world. The wasted gesture acquires a meaning and a context. *In a Free State* plays on 'free states' in order to discover the only freedom that man can own with dignity, that of possessing his own awareness--and watching himself grow--as it alters, expands and contracts responding to experience.

In the extracts from the journal the steamer and the tourist rest house near Luxor are 'no man's land,' for, temporarily social and political restrictions are suspended for their inhabitants. No decisions have to be made or action initiated. The passengers on the steamer, whether there for pleasure or in anxiety, cannot do much

152

except wait. The steamer is either a temporary security or a convenience for people for whom nationality (home) is a confusing or at best an indifferent issue. There are the refugee Greeks who were Egyptian citizens deported to Greece and now reentering Egypt as tourists; the Lebanese businessmen, whose main business is 'frankly money' wherever they can make it; Spanish night club dancers on a similar business and Egyptian students returning from Germany; the tramp, who has been travelling for thirty-eight years, having a fair knowledge of distinctive national traits, yet says:

> But what's nationality these days? I myself, I think of myself as a citizen of the world. (9)

For these people the concept of home has lost some of its original force but they still seek to create centres of the security it implied. They converse in a mixture of languages and accents, their own and acquired. It is the incongruity of this gathering that strikes the narrator. Together, they do not form a community, nor do they stand out as individuals. They congregate in temporary groupings, distinguishable racially, as a crowd, seeking idle entertainment. Whatever the purpose of the journey the people on the upper deck mean to enjoy themselves and the tramp becomes a focus of attention by his odd, self-conscious and solitary appearance:

> It was to be like a tiger-hunt, where bait is laid out and the hunter and spectators watch from the security of a platform. The bait here was the tramp's own rucksack. . . . But Hans smiled and explained the rules of the game as often as he was asked.
>
> The tramp, though, didn't immediately play, Hans remained at his post. . . .
>
> Then the news came that the tramp had reappeared and had been caught according to the rules of the game. (15)

For the refugees crowded on the lower deck the steamer is also literally no man's land. Nationality means security and they mean

153

to acquire one as soon as possible:

> They had the slack bodies and bad skins of people who ate too many carbohydrates. Their blotched faces were immobile, distant, but full of fierce, foolish cunning. They were watching. As soon as the officials came aboard the refugees began to push and fight their way towards them. It was a factitious frenzy, the deference of the persecuted to authority. (19)

Similarly the rest house at Luxor is a no man's land catering to all irrespective of nationality. Money is the only criterion of importance. People who congregate here are all tourists who have no stakes in the land and have left behind all notions of social responsibility and humanity in their own countries. Out for pleasure they are in a 'free state.' The rich tourists, constituting the world of the poor Arab child, are indifferent to his horrifying condition. In mocking him they mock themselves.

The enforced 'free state' of Santosh, Dayo's brother and Bobby brings only an awareness of negative existence: survival at its bare minimum. Loss of an identity leaves them as no man's land. Santosh, having once been 'a part of the flow' discovers an initial identity through his reflection in the mirror, seeing himself as the hubshi woman sees him, as an attractive man. Besides this he discovers other freedom/identifies through other peoples's eyes (his employer, Priya) of money, status, achievement and citizenship of U.S.A. Pursuing other peoples's definitions of freedom and self he discovers that he has gained what other men desire at the cost of a loss of an older ideational identity. Marriage to the hubshi woman is an extreme self-degradation from which he is unable to recover:

> I am a simple man who decided to act and see for himself, and it is as though I have had several lives. . . . Soul Brother. I understand the words; but I feel, brother to what or to whom? I was once part of the flow, never thinking of myself as a presence. Then I looked in the mirror and decided to be free.

154

All that my freedom has brought me is the knowledge that I
have a face and have a body, that I must feed this body and
clothe this body for a certain number of years. Then it will be
over. (57-58)

Despiritualized, for the only dimension to his past life as a servant
has been a religious one, he feels non-existent, in a free state, dead
before he has actually died. The spark of life that remains illuminates the trap of doubt, regret and humiliation into which he has
fallen and it urges him to repossess his self and the world through
reflection, trying to establish a continuity between an imagined and
an actual situation. The maximum freedom available to the San-
toshs of the third world is freedom from economic and social
pressures: the knowledge and nourishment of the body.

For Dayo's brother insanity is the freedom which is available
from a too harsh, too complex reality. His journey to attend Dayo's
marriage to an alien, fraught with the pain of separation and a final
breach with a meaningful existence, a final unimportance, is made
bearable by withdrawal into a world of his own creation in which
he journeys unsystematically through a happier past life. Past and
present, Dayo and Frank, West Indies and London, collapse coalesce and become interchangeable in his confused consciousness.
His resolution, courage and faith have given way under pressure of
loss of hard-earned money and disillusionment at Dayo's abuse of
his love. His moments of sanity (dignity and selfhood) coincide
with the recurring image of Dayo's earlier attractiveness and the
recurring reminder of the purpose of the present journey to attend
Dayo's wedding. The one had given meaning to his life, the latter
breaking off his last links with any desire to live: condemned for
ever to a 'free state,' utterly destitute, unable to form new ties. For
Frank does not understand; he himself has broken links with his
family after his sickness and he has finally realized the temporal
reality of Dayo's love:

I know that he love me, that now it is true, but that it will not
be true as soon as he go out of this room, that he will have to

155

forget me. Because it was my idea after my trouble that nobody should know, that the message should go back home and I was dead. And for all this time I am the dead man. (102)

Paradoxically the affluent, stable colonial life of Bobby and his like is rudely disorganized by independence. Civil War has torn the country apart and no one knows for whom he is working. There is the king, the President and the haunting presence of the colonial master, the white man. Having freely discarded their European identity in sympathy with the 'natives' the expatriates discover they have nowhere to go, rejected and regarded suspiciously by both societies. The 'civilization' they opted for was illusory, imagined and a mockery of Africa and Europe. For Bobby and Linda the once familiar land becomes strange and hostile as they journey through it, as they note each aspect afresh with a growing sense of danger. At each stage of the journey an illusion is discarded regarding the past and white superiority leaving them exposed and vulnerable. Finally the absurdity of Bobby's humiliation at the hands of the President's soldiers at the police outpost to what had once been the king's territory, strips him of his last trace of an established superior identity out to help an under-developed country. He appears as ludicrous and as unbelievably a puppet-like figure as the naked Africans running by the roadside--hardly real. Deprived of the supports of culture and civilization what matters is how fast one can run for shelter in order to survive. There in the shelter the final shock awaits Bobby. The absolute security becomes temporary as the houseboy, responding to the political temper of his tribe, turns 'cheeky.' Bobby's unconscious return to the role of the colonial master in his determination to dismiss the African houseboy is a final submission to a despised past and the loss of a carefully nurtured self. The white bachelor master-black servant relationship of love and loyalty was a unique feature of the colonial civilization. Having lost this, Bobby has nothing further to lose. These white expatriates in the third world, expiating for the colonial authoritarianism of their fathers by seeking equality with the African, find themselves rejected by both, living on the frontiers of both socie-

156

ties. Motivated by some hidden sense of responsibility they end up 'free.' Having travelled through no-man's territory, realizing that in this chaotic state each man was out for himself, their only security is in the moving car or in the compound. It is only when he stops and gets out of his car to walk down to the check-post office that Bobby realizes his mistake. Safety is in keeping moving. When a 'dead-end' is reached journeys are recreated to give a sense of life and purpose. Bobby knows that he will have to leave. Till then, as a safety measure, he will have to do without Luke, his houseboy.

The narrator, journeying literally on the steamer and with the tourist group in Egypt and figuratively with the protagonists of the three stories, never identifies himself. In neither account from the journal does the narrator state his nationality or purpose for the journey. His journal is not dated. Uninvolved and unnoticed he observes, notes and ruminates. His style of writing is 'free,' without any commitment to form or philosophy. This 'free state' is unintentionally lost in a moment of involved action, to be replaced by despair, a vision and a novel.

In *In a Free State* we see people who, having travelled linearly, have arrived at the limits of their known world with "no other place to drive to." (234) Having shed their past and with no further pressure of the future they are in the present in a 'free state.' No man can live consistently in the present as no man can face continuously the glare of the searchlight. Reality is lighted up intermittently as by the steamer's searchlight in *A Bend in the River*. Man exists not only by facing the present directly but by approaching it obliquely, negating its force by moving backwards and forwards in time. A fresh perspective on the present makes the past seem a freer state. Linking present indignity to a past dignity through reflection makes the present pain and humiliation bearable. Having attained an economically free state they discover its ironical, paradoxical contexts--the iron hand in the velvet glove. Freed from their immediate problems they are also freed from their immediate contexts as well. Trapped in contingency, searching for existence they are temporarily stranded in non-existence. The whole movement of Santosh's reflections and Dayo's brother's ruminations follows this pattern. Bobby, not really knowing whether he is moving backwards or forwards, away from or towards safety, finding a friendly landscape turning hostile at every stage of the journey, finally insulted by the person closest to him, finds safety in non-existence, in reverting to a role from being an individual. The 'free state' of the narrator of the journal soon evolves into the stricter role of the narrator/artist of the novel. The requirements of his art and his purpose set limits on his subject matter and restrict logically the narrative horizon of the novel. The reader has the vision of a `trapped' freedom, an anonymity sought and achieved.

The reader may read each of the episodes for its own value. He can view the lives of Santosh, Dayo's brother, Bobby and Linda empathetically as extraordinary, isolated case histories. But he is compelled to interpret the book in terms of the meaning given to these stories by the prologue and the epilogue and perspectivize his interpretation through the experience of the narrator/artist. Thus the reader's final vision of *In a Free State* is controlled by the artist's.

Naipaul establishes, by manipulating the structural devices available to the novelist, a new form for the novel which places it in the mainstream of a man's life making it a necessary experience. Every man is a narrator and the germ of an artistic vision is nascent in the art of narration. As stated earlier he relates the external and internal realities of the protagonist and narrator through the prologue and the epilogue. The narrator submerges after the prologue to re-emerge in the epilogue as a man with a developing vision who mobilizes his materials and tools to shape a unique novel out of his despair. Thus the state of tramphood--the free state of anonymity/ non-existence--is concretized in the episodes and universalized in the form of the novel. Interpretation becomes more important than the story, and the fictive world, no longer revolving around the consciousness of the protagonist only, no longer remains within the pages of a book. Naipaul establishes a complex relationship between the protagonist, narrator, artist and reader, each one viewing an experience from overlapping positions which like varying wavelengths illuminate its different facets.

Below the surface of contingent reality and technical variety, one sees the developing novel possessing the requisites of coherence, sequence and imaginative truth. As is evident coherence, in Naipaul's fiction, does not reside in the consistent use of a single point of view either first or third person. Sequence is not chronological or subjective time and imaginative truth is not a flash of the eternal or transcendent. Coherence in Naipaul's fiction is a function of bias. The bias of his protagonists and narrators is presented as limitation of vision suggested by the limits of their experience, ambition and power of expression. Hence limitation becomes a condition of alienation, loneliness and despair. The protagonists's and narrators's powers to conceive and express are linked positively to their experiences which they try to over-reach but cannot transcend. (His characters do not alter radically by the end of the novel.) Sequence is more of a syntagmatic rather than a paradigmatic progression in his fiction. Certain similar ways of thinking, feeling and acting occur in totally unrelated peoples, cultures and situations enabling him to weave together as wide a geographical tapestry as he has done in *In a Free State*. Imaginative truth is the artist's vision possessed by the reader through recreative analysis. It is a momentary isolated truth which becomes eternal only because it leaves a lasting impression on the mind and is embodied in a work of art. Apart from the work of art this truth had no existence remaining a gesture locked in the mind of the protagonist--in a free state, unpossessed. The children being whipped are only puzzled when the narrator snatches the whip from the Egyptian server:

The two Italians, fingering cameras, looked quite calm behind their sunglasses. The women in the party leaned back in their chairs to consider me.

I felt exposed, futile, and wanted only to be back at my table. When I got back I took up my sandwich. It had happened quickly; there had been no disturbance. . . .

The children remained where they were. The man from whom I had taken the whip came to give me coffee. . . . The coffee was free; . . . But even while he was talking the children

159

had begun to come closer. Soon they would be back, raking the sand for what they had seen the Italian throw out.

I didn't want to see that. The driver was waiting, leaning against the car door, his bare arms crossed.... I was expecting some gesture, some sign of approval. . . . He crushed his cigarette in the sand and slowly breathed out smoke through his lips; he sighed. But that was his way of smoking. I couldn't tell what he thought. He was as correct as before, he looked as bored. (244)

Thematically the title story of *In a Free State* anticipates *Guerrillas* and *A Bend in the River*. All three deal with the personal and social implications of political instability and power politics. Political power is not sought for its own sake as an assertion of national freedom. Eventually the deprived of the third world are beginning to realize that political power is the only tool of successful aggressive activity in defense of the self. And guerrilla tactics in war and politics is the only means of exercising a threatening control over powers--black and white, colonial and expatriate-- which would push them back into colonial servitude. The metaphor is: hunt or be hunted.

In a Free State presents a different argument to the rest of Naipaul's fiction. Dialectically this novel stands alone as an effective question mark to the rest of his fiction. So far his novels have developed in detail situations of entrapment: entrapped individuals seeking release from intense immediate pressure which forbids any idea of the future or of freedom. In each case it is the narrator who raises the question: what does freedom mean in the context of the lives of Ganesh, Harbans Singh, Biswas, Mr. Stone, Ralph Singh, Jimmy and Salim? The narrator emphasizes the hardly measurable distance the protagonist has moved in this direction because of the narrowness of his vision-- "between attic and basement," "pleasure and its penalty" as Ralph Singh says. Yet he highlights the dignity of the effort as a moment of insight against a lengthy and vividly evoked landscape which is dead or disruptive of creativity. The houses that Biswas moves through are metaphors of entrapment. Contrastingly hardly much space has been allotted to the house in Sikkim street which meant release. A major metaphor of entrapment in *The Mimic Men* is the houses and boarding house rooms in which Ralph Singh spends a large part of his life. The hotel room in which he finds a sense of release at the end of the novel received cursory attention. Similarly Mr. Stone's house, for the larger part of the novel, conveys the impression of a prison. The narrator gives only a paragraph at the end describing it as the setting for a Mr. Stone who enters his house with a feeling of release and love for the black cat.

It is easy enough to analyse traps through the wisdom of hindsight. But what does it mean to be free? Can one truly express oneself in any situation without restraint? (This is a contradiction in terms for 'en situation' defines its own restraints of time and place). So far as the narrator/artist can see to be free in the existing situation is an unenviable condition. For, to be free like Santosh, Dayo's brother and Bobby, without a wider vision than that of the self, is to be trapped in the self as one was earlier by circumstance, for it leads back only to one's own past. In *In a Free State* we see the protagonist arriving at successive stages of being free from anxiety. Each free situation carries its own disillusionments. Each creates its own insecurities and necessitates further movement to the very limits of the literal and the literary in each context. "In a Free State" describes in detail Bobby's sense of security and freedom of action. The incident in the bar at the New Shropshire with the Zulu elaborates the gestures of a man at ease in his environment. The setback he receives when the Zulu boy spits at him does not disturb him unduly:

Africa was for Bobby the empty spaces, the safe adventures of long fatiguing drives on open roads, the other Africans, boys built like men. 'You want lift? You big boy, you no go school? . . . When I born again I want your colour. You no frighten. You want five shillings?' (109)

That evening he had broken all rules; the evening had shown how right his rules were. He felt no bitterness, no hurt.

161

He didn't blame the Zulu, he didn't blame Linda. Before Africa, the incident of the evening might have driven him out adventuring for hours more in dangerous places; ... But now he knew that the mood would pass; the morning would come. Even with Linda as his passenger, the drive remained. (110)

Throughout the journey, till the very end, Bobby and Linda are travel companions, sensitive to sights and sounds, indulging freely in light conversation, aware of each feeling as it passes through their minds. Bobby ignores or suppresses all impressions of impending danger. As Bobby and Linda move into the future, the new unknown Africa, his sense of insecurity deepens till they are almost in a panic to reach the safety of the compound. Hardly two pages are ascribed to the description of this safety which is part of the trap into which Bobby falls and from which it will be hard for him to release himself; Bobby's unconscious assumption of the role of the colonial master is not very relevant in his context: he has shifted into a world as fragile and exposed as that outside the compound:

> Bobby thought: I will have to leave. But the compound was safe; the soldiers guarded the gate. Bobby thought: I will have to sack Luke. (238)

Similarly Santosh's and Dayo's brother's sense of release is enlarged upon in the contextual setting rather than their traps till a final 'free' state is the trap of the alienated subjective life.

Finality for the narrator is the ultimate trap. He depicts each protagonist in a final state from which the narrator releases him through story-telling. The despair of literal limits (of the void, of death) is counteracted by literary movement. Self-awareness adds the dimension of dignity to their personalities. We appreciate these failed men who can live with the knowledge of failure like the Egyptian soldiers on their way home from Sinai, "lost, trying to walk back home, casting long shadows on the sand." (246) The narrator of the epilogue sees himself as one such. Release, then, for the narrator is in the art of narration and in having an Idea. The demands of precision, order and semantics situates the end of the narrative in the beginning. And the Idea, separating from existence, becoming an abstraction, ends up as an absurdity. Both these requirements place restraints on the freedom of the narrator. For the artist, seeing the world as paradox, the greatest trap is the temptation to inaction and the highest free state is to reexamine an Idea and to act; to write another book.

The question raised by an overview of Naipaul's fiction, in which the fictive parameters are guided by considerations of entrapment and release, is what is the relationship between being trapped, being in a free state and the idea of freedom. Philosophically and psychologically this can be restated as having a fresh look at the relationship that exists between existence, absurdity and self-awareness on the one hand and abstraction, freedom and non-existence on the other. Abstractions, urging a man in unknown directions, have 'existed,' if at all, in the past. For abstraction engages the concepts of oneness, wholeness, purity and innocence which, as permanent features of life today are beyond definition. They are the artist's vision of the past (245) which suggest 'nothing' for the future. Absurdity, both as existential anguish in the face of the void and the rational awareness of irony (the outer limits of subjectivity and objectivity) is the great turning point or dividing line where the trapped protagonist unites in his self-awareness, however briefly and lightly, the frontiers of freedom/abstraction with existence. Absurdity is a virtue and man's saving grace in Naipaul's fiction, promising the only freedom available today for his third world characters: that of growing individuation, whose parameters are limitless, outwards towards the world and inwards by reflecting in it. Thus entrapped and free states become conditions of awareness, ranging from the literal to the literary, and are not unalterables known and examined independently of the protagonist's existence.

We see the absurdity that is despair most vividly in Salim's condition. We see the absurdity that is the free state of non-existence portrayed in Mr. Stone: a monument to habit. The naked tribal Africans running at the edge of the road, viewed by Bobby in his moving car, are not only mirage-like but, if yet existent, render modern Africa an absurdity. The tramp, wandering meaninglessly round the globe, lives on the margin between existence and non-existence, a character with whom the narrator can readily empathize--aware of the world, wanting but unable to be a part of it.

Naipaul's little man is seen as one who makes great efforts, in spite of his almost insurmountable handicaps, to realign himself to an ill-defined present, ending up as a failure either in his own estimation or in that of his narrator. Hence Naipaul is considered to be a pessimist and is said to have a poor view of man. But this is a sweeping judgment of his fiction. His vision is focussed on a particular third world reality--the homeless man in search of an identity which dignifies. That he fails is also a particular truth of his situation today. But the fact that Naipaul's most endurable and lovable characters are travellers and explorers, that he uses the tools of analysis to sift for man's possibilities is an impossible world, that none of his protagonists ever commits suicide, is sufficient evidence of Naipaul's faith in humanity. What everyone's private heaven or hell is, is not his concern for no one can know another's existential anguish. But the fact that they face it distinguishes the individual from a faceless society. His protagonists, like Bunyan's pilgrims, are to be admired on the journey.

And it is in his next novel *The Enigma of Arrival*, that Naipaul's protagonist, grown worldly wise, ponders on the personal implications of the journeys he has undertaken. He examines the paradox of ceremonial departures and unheralded arrivals. Consciously leaving behind a world in which he is someone, certain that great things lie ahead, he arrives, unknown and insecure and builds a second life for himself. He has arrived. But for reasons of ill-health he has to move again. So, ironically, the arrival has only led to the preparation for another departure.

N O T E S

1.   V.S. Naipaul, *In a Free State* (Harmondsworth: Penguin, 1978), p. 246.

The Enigma of Arrival:
The Limits of the Novel

The narrator-protagonist of *The Enigma of Arrival,* an autobiographical novel, is a writer. The novel is in five parts--two parts
describe events in the writer's life which 'seed' its three remaining
parts.

The novel opens with the protagonist-narrator ruminating on
his arrival at his retreat in the cottage in the grounds of the
Waldenshaw estate in the valley of the Avon river, near the town of
Salisbury in Wiltshire. He is a stranger to the locality with the raw
nerves and extreme self-consciousness of a newcomer.

The novel dramatises a period of just over ten years of his life
in this cottage and ends with his move to another house, a short
distance away, which he has restructured out of two shepherds's
cottages.

It describes minutely a rural landscape incongruently aware
of industrial life and modernity-farm machinery, refrigerated tanks
for collection of milk, milking machines, modern storage bins,
mechanised transport, pre-fabricated sheds, artillery ranges lumi-
nous orange in the sunlight and farmers who look like industrial
workers in haphazard company with dilapidated barns, decaying
hay ricks, shepherds's cottages, rutted muddy roads, crude methods
of cattle rearing and sheep shearing. And against all this is Jack and
his garden and the ancient circle of the Stonehenge, the tall beeches,
elms, sycamores and oaks--the beauty of the natural landscape.

The protagonist, leading a bachelor's lonely existence, cherishes his solitude as a period of respite and recovery from tragic
experience--the death of his sister Sati in far away Trinidad and the

rejection of a book by a publisher who had commissioned him to write it.

The publisher had wanted a travel guide to a Caribbean island, but he had written it 'sincerely,' researching into its history to discover its transformation into a British colony. Apart from the financial strain, this rejection is a negation of the writer's personality and task. At present he is writing a book about a region in Africa:

> And then the healing starts with his writer's sense of curiosity, mystery and beauty aroused by the first few days of rain and mist and the world hidden from view.
> And when the rain stopped and the mist lifted, after those first four days, I went out one afternoon, looking for the walk and the view.'
> The four days of rain and mist that hid my surroundings from me and answered my anxiety at the time, anxiety about my work and this move to a new place. (13)

The countryside entices the protagonist to wander over hills and downs and in the river valleys, through plantations of beech, elm and oak. Its pre-historic mounds and tumult excite the writer's imagination about the people who lived then. He sees the Stonehenge and the artillery range, the ancient past and the modern world, in the same visual field.

He sees the farming, gardening, dairy and farmyard activities on his walks and begins to view the men and women who can make a successful living on that chalky, flinty soil, more closely. Jack's garden speaks to him of Jack.

> It was Jack's garden that made me notice Jack. . . . The people in the other cottages I never got to know, couldn't recognise, never knew when they moved in or moved out. But it took some time to see the garden. So many weeks, so many walks between the whitish chalk and flint hills. . . .
> I noticed his hedge first of all . . . and everything he tended

answered the special idea he had of that thing. . . . (20-22)

The novel develops as dramatic episodes in the life of the protagonist-narrator as he encounters different people in his daily routine. He observes them in their own surroundings--at labour and recreation. He sees them in harmony with 'the earth they walk on.' He observes their commitment. This fills up the empty spaces in his own being and he finds tranquillity in this imagined state of finite human perfection.

> My wonder at the satisfactions of his life . . . a man in his own setting, as I thought (to me an especially happy condition), a man in tune with the seasons and his landscape. (33)
> I had found in that beard of his, and in his bearing, his upright, easy, elegant walk, the attributes of a man with a high idea of himself a man who had out of principle turned away from other styles of life. (32)

In Jack's garden he sees the primal Eden and Jack is the original artist and, in his own third world context, the first Aryan horseman riding to the edge of the flat world. But Jack's death and the consequent neglect of the garden makes himself speak of the finiteness of human perfection and he begins to attach significance to change and flux in human life. Though Jack is dead his wife is alive--she has bobbed her hair and re-married. He seeks to understand him in terms of his surroundings. In Jack's story he sees his own possible perfections and also his death which will annihilate those perfections.

In his landlord, the lord of the manor, who loves ivy even when it destroys the trees it grows on, he sees another kind of security--the security of a parasite. He writes about the Phillipses, caretakers of the manor house, and their servant mentality which aspires to the pretensions of manor house society. They are like the ivy--they grow on the lord--and monitor his contact with the outside world. They cater to his love of seclusion and an unchanging 'perfect' world.

167

In Pitton the gardener, Bray the car-hire man and in Stan Phillips's father, past his working life, the protagonist-narrator experiences in varied ways that dignity which a man achieves when his work becomes his vocation. Their pride in their work and confidence in their capability give them roots--make them humane. They are not afraid to judge, criticise, sympathise and love. And when the environment becomes unsuitable they are not afraid to get up and go. They take change and death in their stride as they strive to live fully while they are living.

Thus, as he experiences the death or departure of his relations, friends and acquaintances, sees plants and flowers die with the change of the seasons, sees trees grow, give shade and shelter and die, he becomes aware, in a subtle way, that all that is anonymous also leaves a mark on its environment. His friends have left their mark on him as he writes of them from memory. They have left their mark on the environment. In their absence the small, stable worlds they created alter and are never the same again:

> This gate hung unevenly, but Pitton had developed the knack of closing it. His successors didn't have this knack. The gate, unlatched, dragged more and more and was eventually left open: Pitton's garden, the scene of his secret labours, now quite exposed. . . . Pitton had been able to keep only part of the garden going; but he had honoured its formality, design and dignity. Now, after the bonanza of his vegetable garden, his successors were creating only an allotment.
>
> A cycle in the life of the manor had come to an end. There might one day be the beginning of a new cycle. (249)

And the same will happen with him.

Thus the protagonist-narrator, when he eventually writes the novel, creates a melancholy mood--nostalgic for the moment of perfection actually experienced which has passed away. Such experiences enable him to pull himself after each defeat to start on another journey.

The narrator-protagonist as the writer of *The Enigma of*

Arrival has exercised (with the restraint of an artist) his imagination and empathy to create a microcosm in and around Waldenshaw which reflects the finer moods of life and death. Underlying this sublimated world, suggested in the imagery, is the animal world of human brutality, violence, decay, indifference and death. He dramatizes his characters trying to keep this world at bay, most frequently by ignoring it as long as they can. In their private Edens there is no recognition of this evil aspect of human activity:

> Cows and grass and trees: pretty country views--they existed all around me. . . .
>
> Now, not far from that view, there was this intimate act of cruelty. The memory of that mutilated, bleeding pony, still with the bad-tempered toss of its head and mane, being led to the white gate below the yews by the two big-headed men, father and son, was with me for some time. (38)
>
> Jack himself had disregarded the tenuousness of his hold on the land, just as, not seeing what others saw, he had created a garden on the edge of a swamp and a ruined farmyard. . . . All around him was ruin; and all around, in a deeper way, was change. . . . But he had sensed that life and man were the true mysteries: and he had asserted the primacy of these with something like religion. (87)

The country setting of the Edwardian manor house surrounded by hamlets and farms, woods, country roads (so that the occasional car, bus, tanker and other forms of automation almost assumed a rural character), the typical characters who people it all suggest a novel of manners. But the narrator-protagonist's identity as a stranger from another world and a writer (in a society which looks on writing as an aristocratic pastime) subverts the chronology of the novel of manners. The writer, a character in his own novel, compulsively probes the psyches of his characters, hoping thereby to resolve his own dilemmas.

It is a novel of moods. It is the writer's mood of discovery of places, people, the passage of time and finally death, which govern his choice of episodes and their repetitive occurrence in fresh contexts throughout the novel. For, as the writer says, no journey is truly linear when one travels with one's eyes and ears open. A physical journey may be undertaken only once but imaginatively a writer travels over the same route many times and each journey is slightly different from all previous ones. Previously unnoticed or ignored objects and aspects of a familiar environment come to life acquiring different hues.

The remote English countryside, unknown people living uneventful lives, acquire the power of meaning through the vision and skill of the protagonist-narrator-writer. Events, scenes and people remind the writer of earlier events, scenes and people off-stage of the novel he is writing. There are flash-backs to actual happenings in the life of V.S. Naipaul. As these later seed the events in the novel the autobiographical element becomes an important source of meaning too. The insignificant setting and common characters can bear the weight of the protagonist-narrator's preoccupation with death, with fear of change, his search for human values in a vulgar and mean existence only because they are placed within the autobiographical context of his tragic disillusionments.

The extent to which the autobiographical element remains constant in all Naipaul's fiction is evident in certain metaphors which occur fairly frequently. The metaphors of entrapment and the journey undertaken to escape the constricting influence of such situations encapsulates Naipaul's fiction so that the third world protagonist's anguish of homelessness is pressed upon the consciousness of the audience.

The Enigma of Arrival is, however, full of surprises. It is the metaphor of the journey that becomes prominent: the fear of entrapment recedes. The protagonist knows that the journey he undertakes into the Wiltshire countryside is different from all previous journeys--it is an arrival with a difference. It is a changed man who, though excited about his new surroundings, yet exercises restraint and caution in interpreting them as they are in themselves and how they matter to him.

The arrival point of his earlier journeys was pre-determined

170

by the context of his upbringing in mean Trinidad. The world of Western civilization, known secondhand through school texts and later literature, was already a glorified version of reality. This vision was further enhanced by the imaginative yearning of the writer for his ideal setting. The 'island innocent' is, however, disillusioned on arrival at the land of his imagination. The sameness and ordinariness of life everywhere leaves him annulled. The only recovery is to travel once more to continue searching for a 'resting place for the imagination.'

This arrival in Waldenshaw is a new life because he comes here having faced the final annullment--the deaths of those he has valued. It is nature's laws of dying and rejuvenation, as the seasons change, that awaken in him the existential understanding that it is the completeness of living in the moment that reduces the fear of death:

> though the farm was set among ruins of many sorts, reminders of the impermanence of men's doings, there was another side to men's work. Men came back, men went on, men did and did again. How small the caravels were that crossed the Atlantic and intruded into the evenness of history on the other side; how few the men in those small vessels, how limited their means; how barely noticed. But they went back. They changed the world in that part forever. (44)

And so this stranger in a new land has arrived in many ways and he is contented. He is able to appreciate the paradox of arrivals and departures as in the painting by Chirico, given the title *The Enigma of Arrival* by the poet Appllinaire. He then writes his novel of the same name, seeing a certain ironical reflection of his own situation in this painting.

Interwoven through this autobiographical novel is an implicit statement about the beginnings and endings of novels. Having developed the metaphors for his novel from actual journeys and deaths--from which this novel generated--the writer describes different openings for his novel. These range from a classical

171

Roman setting to the one he has actually written about--his arrival in Wiltshire and Jack's garden. The novel's beginnings are seen to be influenced by many extraneous factors and change with the writer's mood or circumstances. But the ending is more or less predetermined.

In *The Enigma of Arrival* there is an underlying sense of the genre of the novel as a closed form. There is only one possible ending to every story--death itself. It may be prolonged, it may not actually occur in the story, but the foreboding of its finality guides the novelist's story to the end.

> At the moment of crisis he would come upon a door, open it, and find himself back on the quayside of arrival. He has been saved: the world is as he remembered it. Only one thing is missing now. Above the cut-out walls and buildings there is no mast, no sail. The antique ship has gone. The traveller has lived out his life. (92)

Though in this novel there are many deaths, but not even one harrowing deathbed scene has been described. Yet the writer succeeds in creating an enveloping melancholy which pervades all other moods in the novel including the comic vision of the protagonist-narrator whose achievement is that he has found an actual haven of peace and tranquillity in men and their landscapes.

This story then professes the novel as a closed form when it projects the tragi-comic existence of contemporary man. The protagonist-narrator-writer is witness to the events and the tragi-comic characters of this story. Though these characters lack humour they have acquired dignity because of their faith in their labour and its fruits.

NOTES

1. V.S. Naipaul, *The Enigma of Arrival* (Harmondsworth: Penguin, 1987), pp. 11-12.

Index

174